Photo by Joan Marcus

A scene from the Arena Stage production of *Ourselves Alone*. Set and costume designs by Annie Smart.

OURSELVES ALONE

BY ANNE DEVLIN

★

DRAMATISTS
PLAY SERVICE
INC.

OURSELVES ALONE
Copyright © 1986, 1990, 1999, Anne Devlin

All Rights Reserved

SPECIAL NOTE

For Chris Parr with love

OURSELVES ALONE was produced by Arena Stage (Zelda Fichandler, Producing Director; William Stewart, Managing Director; Douglas C. Wager, Associate Producing Director) in Washington, D.C., on March 20, 1987. It was directed by Les Waters; the set and costume designs were by Annie Smart; the lighting design was by Nancy Schertler; the sound design was by Susan R. White; the vocal consultant was Richard Ericson; and the stage manager was Wendy Streeter. The cast was as follows:

DANNY .... John Leonard
FRIEDA .... Heather Ehlers
GABRIEL, LIAM, SECOND SOLDIER ...... Christopher McHale
FIRST MAN, FIRST POLICEMAN ....Marty Lodge
JOSIE ....Randy Danson
DONNA .... Christina Moore
MALACHY ....Terrence Currier
JOE CONRAN .... Robert Westernberg
JOHN McDERMOT ....Thomas Anthony Quinn
FIRST SOLDIER, SECOND POLICEMAN ....Jason Adams
CATHAL O'DONNELL ....John Finn

OURSELVES ALONE was co-produced at the Liverpool Playhouse Studio, in London, on October 24, 1985, and at the Royal Court Theatre Upstairs, in London, on November 20, 1985. It was directed by Simon Curtis; the design was by Paul Brown. The cast was as follows:

DANNY .... Liam de Staic
FRIEDA .... Hilary Reynolds
GABRIEL .... Mark Lambert
JOSIE ....Brid Brennan
DONNA .... Lise-Ann McLaughlin
MALACHY.. John Hewitt
JOE CONRAN .... Peter Chelson
JOHN McDERMOT, CATHAL O'DONNELL ....Adrian Dunbar
All other parts played by the Company.

4

OURSELVES ALONE was transferred to The Royal, mainstage, in August, 1986, on the first leg of the Dublin Theatre Festival tour. The cast was as follows:

DANNY... Owen O'Callaghan
FRIEDA .... Sylvestra Le Touzel
GABRIEL, LIAM .... B.J. Hogg
JOSIE...Fiona Victory
DONNA.. Aingael Grehan
MALACHY.. John Hewitt
JOE CONRAN .... Michael Feast
JOHN McDERMOT, CATHAL O'DONNELL ....Melissa Stafford

AUTHOR'S NOTE

I began this play with two women's voices — one funny and one serious — and then I found I had a third — the voice of a woman listening. And all the women were in some ways living without men. And then the father and a stranger came into the room. And I found myself wondering who the stranger was and what he was doing there. And I set the play in Andersonstown because once, I used to live there — and I still do.

August 1985

CHARACTERS

FRIEDA — Sister to Josie, under 25 years
JOSIE — Sister to Frieda, under 29 years
DONNA — Friend to both sisters, Liam's common-law wife, under 30
MALACHY — Father to Frieda, Josie and Liam
LIAM — Malachy's son, Donna's common-law husband
GABRIEL — Cousin to Frieda, Josie and Liam
JOE CONRAN — The Englishman
CATHAL O'DONNELL — Josie's lover, a member of the Provisional IRA
JOHN McDERMOT — A member of the Workers' Party
DANNY McLOUGHLIN — A musician
FIRST MAN — A helper in the Club
SECOND MAN — In the fight outside the Club
FIRST POLICEMAN — In the park, and in Donna's house
SECOND POLICEMAN — In the park
FIRST SOLDIER — In Donna's house
SECOND SOLDIER — In Donna's house

TIME

Act One is set in late summer; Act Two autumn into winter. Duration: eight months.

SETTING

Mainly Andersonstown, West Belfast; but also Dublin, a hotel room, and John McDermot's house in South Belfast, near the university and the Botanic Gardens.

7

OURSELVES ALONE

ACT ONE

Scene 1

Frieda, Danny, Gabriel, First Man. The setting is a club, the centre of Republican activity, political and social, in West Belfast. The period of Republicanism in the post-hunger-strike days is set by the wall hangings; the traditional prominence of Pearse and Connolly has given way to the faces in black and white of ten men: Sands, Hughes, McCreesh, O'Hara, McDonnell, Hurson, Lynch, Doherty, McElwee, Devine.

It is early evening, the lights in the Club are down, the surroundings are not so visible. Frieda, a singer, and Danny, a musician, are rehearsing.

FRIEDA. *(Sings.)*
    Armoured cars and tanks and guns
    came to take away our sons
    every man should stand beside
    the men behind the wire.
(Throws the paper down.)
    I don't want to sing this any more!
(Behind them and around them two men are coming in and out with boxes and stacking them in every available space.)
DANNY. *(Stops playing.)* Why not?
FRIEDA. Because it's about a man.
DANNY. The song's about Internment, Frieda!
FRIEDA. I'm fed up with songs where the women are doormats!
DANNY. It's a Republican classic!

9

FRIEDA. I want to sing one of my own songs.

DANNY. But your songs are — not as popular as this one.

FRIEDA. You told me the next time we got a job here you'd let me sing one of my own songs! Just one.

DANNY. *(Sighs.)* Which one did you want to sing?

FRIEDA. I've rewritten "The Volunteer." *(She starts getting a paper out of her bag by the piano.)*

DANNY. All right. I'll look at it when we've rehearsed this.

FRIEDA. Oh Danny. I knew you would.

DANNY. OK. Let's go again.

FRIEDA. *(She sings the first verse of "The Men Behind The Wire.")*
　　　Armoured cars and tanks and guns
　　　came to take away our sons —

DANNY. *(Stops.)* Frieda! Do you have to sound so pleased about it? Armoured cars and tanks and guns!

FRIEDA. But the tempo's fast and lively.

DANNY. Absolutely. You have to work hard against that tempo. Again! *(She sings. She stops. The men carrying boxes are now piling them nearer Frieda.)* Just a minute … Are you going to be much longer shifting that stuff around?

GABRIEL. Nearly finished.

FRIEDA. *(Looking into the box Gabriel has put down.)* What is it anyway?

GABRIEL. Bandages.

FRIEDA. In all of them?

GABRIEL. *(Nods.)* I think so. *(The First Man comes in with a larger box, his last.)*

FRIEDA. What are you trying to do — start a fight? *(Calls out.)* Hey wee fella, what have you got in your box?

FIRST MAN. *(Reading off the lid.)* Cotton wool balls.

FRIEDA. I always thought there was something funny about you.

FIRST MAN. *(On his way out.)* See you wee girl, come the revolution, you'll be the first one up against the wall!

FRIEDA. Well, I hope it's in the nicest possible way.

GABRIEL. What were you looking for?

FRIEDA. Sugar.

GABRIEL. Maybe next week.

DANNY. Frieda! *(She clears her throat, takes up her position. The men depart. She sings the song again completely.)*

Scene 2

Donna, Josie, Frieda, Malachy, Joe. Josie is sitting in the dark in a room. Footsteps quickly approach the door. Donna comes in and turns on the light.

DONNA. Josie! What are you doing sitting in the dark? You've let the fire out. *(Josie laughs.)* What's so funny?
JOSIE. My daddy used to say, well close the door quickly and keep it in.
DONNA. Used to say? *(Takes her coat off and sits down.)* You couldn't wait to get away from him.
JOSIE. I know.
DONNA. Is everything all right? You were sleepwalking again last night.
JOSIE. Was I?
DONNA. It's the third time this week. I opened my eyes and there you were. Standing over the cot, looking at Catherine.
JOSIE. Was I?
DONNA. You gave me an awful fright.
JOSIE. I'm sorry.
DONNA. I wouldn't have said anything, but I'm afraid of you waking Catherine. It takes so long to get her to sleep these days.
JOSIE. I think I was dreaming about my mother.
DONNA. Was she quiet for you?
JOSIE. Who?
DONNA. Catherine. Was she quiet while I was out?
JOSIE. Yes.
DONNA. I'll just take a wee look in.
JOSIE. She's asleep! I wish I could sleep like that.
DONNA. What's wrong?
JOSIE. I feel sick all the time now.
DONNA. Is it him?

11

JOSIE.   I can't live like this any more. I sit here night after night wondering will he come tonight.
DONNA.   We're all waiting on men, Josie.
JOSIE.   If he has to go away for any other reason but her I can stand it.
DONNA.   Have you told him this?
JOSIE.   No. Of course not. I don't want him to think I care.
DONNA.   Aye, but it strikes me that if you were the one with a wife, he might care. Has he ever talked about her?
JOSIE.   No.
DONNA.   Well I expect she waits too, Josie.
JOSIE.   Thanks.
DONNA.   At least you have his love.
JOSIE.   Love? It's such a silly word. We've never spoken it. It's just that when I'm totally me and he's totally him we swop. Do you know what I mean? *(Pause.)* His arrival is the best time. It's his mouth on my neck, his cool fingers touching me — I make it last right up until he has to leave. And then I row, I fight, I do everything I can to keep him with me and when I hurt him I hurt myself. It's as if we're driven, that bed is like a raft and that room is all the world to us.
DONNA.   You're lucky you can feel like that, you might not if you had to live with him.
JOSIE.   Live with him? I've dreamt of nothing else.
DONNA.   He frightens me Josie — he's not like any man I know.
JOSIE.   No he's not.
DONNA.   The things I've heard about him. He's a spoiled priest.
JOSIE.   Sure I wanted to be a nun once.
DONNA.   Aye when you were ten years old. But he's actually been trained as a priest. *(Pause.)* They told him when they blew up the police station near the cemetery that morning that some of our people might get hurt as well. And he asked — how many?
JOSIE.   You don't know what you're talking about. Our force is defensive!
DONNA.   I'm looking at you but it's him who's talking. I wish

I didn't know any of this. I wish I hadn't walked into the room that night and seen you both. I wish you hadn't left the door open.

JOSIE.   But you approved of us. You made me come and live with you so it was easier for us to meet. You got me away from my daddy.

DONNA.   I was afraid for you if they found out. And because you have Liam's eyes. When I woke last night I thought it was Liam who was standing there, that he'd come back. But when I saw it was you, I knew it was only because I hadn't been with him for so long I was wanting him again.

JOSIE.   Don't talk to me about wanting, my body's like armour. The nerve ends are screeching under my skin. I need him back so I can stretch out again.

DONNA.   How long since you've seen him?

JOSIE.   Five weeks.

DONNA.   I wonder does she know. *(Pause.)* Women have a way of knowing these things. I knew with my ex-husband when he was seeing somebody else. I knew the minute he put his hand on me. Once when we were in bed together a woman's name came into my head and I thought, he's not making love to me, he's making love to Margaret — I asked him afterwards, who's Margaret? He froze. He was, you see.

JOSIE.   Sometimes when we make love I pretend I'm somebody else.

DONNA.   Who?

JOSIE.   Not someone I know. Someone I make up — from another century. Sometimes I'm not even a woman. Sometimes I'm a man — his warrior lover, fighting side by side to the death. Sometimes we're not even on the same side.

DONNA.   That's powerful, Josie! *(Pause.)* What will you do if he doesn't come back?

JOSIE.   Why do you say that?

DONNA.   The man is still married to someone else. He has known you all these years — but he has never left his wife.

JOSIE.   But she's not important to him!

DONNA.   Wives are always important.

JOSIE.   You only say that because you're so anxious to marry

13

my brother.

DONNA. I must have struck home!

JOSIE. I'm sorry. *(She suddenly stops. Footsteps clattering in the alley towards the door.)* Listen.

DONNA. You've ears like a cat.

JOSIE. It's Frieda. She always walks as if her feet don't belong to her.

DONNA. Here. *(Offers her a hanky.)* Blow your nose. *(The door bursts open. Frieda arrives, breathing deeply. Leans against the closed door.)*

FRIEDA. Oh God!

DONNA. What's wrong?

FRIEDA. I was nearly gang-raped at the Club.

JOSIE. Is that all?

DONNA. Don't do that again. You gave us the fright of our lives. The way you came down that alley.

FRIEDA. I was rehearsing at the Club for the Prisoners' Dependants "do." It was dark and there was only Danny and myself. Danny's a friend of mine, he's a musician.

DONNA. Yes. We know.

FRIEDA. I'd been singing for about an hour when I suddenly looked around and the room was full of men. There'd been one of those meetings upstairs. They must have heard my singing and come down.

JOSIE. Like a siren.

FRIEDA. I'll ignore that. Anyway, Danny sent me home. I was the only woman in the room.

JOSIE. No doubt you made the most of it.

DONNA. Strange there was a meeting and you weren't there.

JOSIE. I'm going out later.

FRIEDA. You'll never guess what I was singing when they came down to listen!

DONNA. I'll never guess.

FRIEDA. My own song. We were rehearsing a song I had written myself.

DONNA. It was that bad, was it? *(Pause.)* I'm only joking. That's great Frieda. That's a break for you.

FRIEDA. Must have been something important going on.

14

Cathal O'Donnell was there. He stopped to talk to me on my way out. He said I'd a great voice. He had that doe-eyed look about him; you know the one — I'm married, please rescue me. I could hardy get away from him.

JOSIE.   O'Donnell's in the north?

FRIEDA.   I think he's been here for a while. I thought I saw him there last week as well. You know how distinctive he looks. He's so lean and dark and brooding.

DONNA.   Are you going to wash your hair tonight? There's plenty of hot water.

FRIEDA.   I am, then I'll do yours.

DONNA.   Good. My roots are beginning to show.

FRIEDA.   *(To Josie.)* Are you all right?

DONNA.   She's got a bit of a cold. Why don't you take your things and go and do your hair now.

FRIEDA.   There's no rush.

DONNA.   There is — I want an early night.

FRIEDA.   She's just said she's got to go out.

DONNA.   I still want an early night.

FRIEDA.   What's wrong with you?

JOSIE.   I've got earache and a sore throat; I haven't had a good night's sleep for a long time.

FRIEDA.   *(Pause.)* Do you know what I thought you said? I haven't had a man to sleep with for a long time.

DONNA.   Frieda! While the water's warm!

FRIEDA.   I'm going. I'm going. *(Frieda exits.)*

DONNA.   Why don't you go and have a sleep before you go out?

JOSIE.   He's here, Donna. He talked to her!

DONNA.   Quick, before she comes back. Sleep in my room. Then you won't have to listen to Frieda all evening.

JOSIE.   Why doesn't he come? Is it her? She says he wants her.

DONNA.   Oh stop it. It's all in Frieda's mind. She doesn't know who to be at!

JOSIE.   I don't know if I could share him.

DONNA.   You're already sharing him! Stop tormenting yourself. Why don't you have a wee sleep before you go out?

JOSIE.   I can't, not now. I'm going to see him in a few hours.

(In the distance the faint sound of bin lids hammering on the pavement.)

DONNA. Bin lids.

JOSIE. Quite far off.

DONNA. Somebody's been lifted.

JOSIE. No doubt. *(They listen again. It seems to get louder.)*

DONNA. Is it getting closer?

JOSIE. No. It's the wind. It's changed direction. *(It stops.)*

DONNA. It makes me nervous. Nights like this. I'm glad Liam's in prison — God forgive me — it means I don't have to lie awake waiting for them to come for him. Listening to every sound. I wouldn't go through that again for anything. *(Sound of helicopter faintly in the background.)*

JOSIE. My mother spent her life listening. My father was picked up four times.

DONNA. Oh, I hope they're not going to raid us. I only got the carpets down at Christmas. I'll never get the doors to close. That happened the last time they came. They pulled up the carpets and half the floorboards. That was after your brother'd been arrested, and I'd no one to help me put them back. *(Bin lids begin faintly again. Frieda opens the door. She is wearing a tinfoil turban.)*

FRIEDA. Well, girls, what do you think — Miss Andersonstown second year running. *(Josie motions her to be quiet. She listens.)* What is it, a raid? It's far enough away. *(They all listen.)* Do you remember the last time you were raided?

DONNA. I was just walking about that.

FRIEDA. It was hardly worth their while. They only found a couple of rounds of ammunition. I remember this place the morning after, though. It was a shambles.

DONNA. Don't remind me. *(The bin lids die.)*

JOSIE. It's stopped.

DONNA. I wish you didn't have to go out again tonight.

FRIEDA. I must say you don't look very well.

JOSIE. I don't look well?

DONNA. *(Eyeing Frieda also.)* What's the tinfoil for?

FRIEDA. They use tinfoil at the salon, I'll be blonde in ten minutes.

16

DONNA.   Why do hairdressers think they always have to be blonde!

FRIEDA.   It's not that. It's for my act. Marlene Dietrich was blonde.

JOSIE.   If you spent as much time on your mind as you do on your appearance you'd be better equipped.

FRIEDA.   For what? I want to be a singer, not an academic.

JOSIE.   A few exam passes might help.

FRIEDA.   How did it help you? You went to university, but you still live in Andersonstown.

JOSIE.   I live here because I choose to.

FRIEDA.   I don't believe you — anyway, Marilyn Monroe didn't pass any exams. *(Donna and Josie laugh.)*

DONNA.   What did I tell you? Monroe! Dietrich! She's a head about herself.

JOSIE.   Why do you always want to be somebody else?

FRIEDA.   I don't always want to be somebody else. I just want to be somebody.

JOSIE.   Be yourself.

FRIEDA.   When did I ever have a chance to be myself? My father was interned before I was born. My brother's in the Kesh for bank robbery. You mention the name McCoy in this neighbourhood, people start walking away from you backwards. I'm fed up living here, this place is a hole!

JOSIE.   If it's a hole, it's a hole for all of us.

FRIEDA.   Yeah, but there's this voice in my head which says "Nobody knows you. Nobody knows you exist. You've got to make yourself known."

JOSIE.   Is that why you've attached yourself to the Workers' Party?

DONNA.   Have you?

JOSIE.   She was seen with them at a dance at Queen's last week.

FRIEDA.   I was talking to John McDermot.

JOSIE.   You were also seen coming out of Maguire's pub on Saturday.

FRIEDA.   I thought that was Gabriel driving off when I waved.

JOSIE.   Maguire's is where the Officials hang out.

17

FRIEDA. You ought to apply to the SAS, Josie. They could use somebody with your intelligence.

JOSIE. You may be my sister, but it won't save you! You're in and out of the Club all the time. You could be carrying information to the Officials.

FRIEDA. I've nothing to do with the Officials. I was talking to John McDermot.

JOSIE. I know you wouldn't talk; but there's others who might point the finger at you. You'll put all of us under suspicion.

DONNA. Josie's right. They're paranoid about informers now. You'll get your family a bad name.

FRIEDA. Could we sink any lower?

JOSIE. I give up with you. Liam's getting out of the Kesh next month; talk to him about it.

FRIEDA. I don't know why you're making such a fuss. John McDermot is an old friend. You used to like him yourself when he was Liam's mate.

JOSIE. Not these days, my girl. The only loyalties you are allowed are ideological.

FRIEDA. Baloney! Look at her! She's not living with an ideology. My brother's changed his political line three times at least since 'sixty-nine. He joined the Officials when they split with the Provos, then the INLA when they split from the Officials; the last time he was out on parole he was impersonating votes for the Sinn Fein election. And I hear lately while he's in the Kesh he's joined the Provos! Now what does that tell us — apart from the fact that he's a relentless political opportunist?

JOSIE. Liam's always been confused!

FRIEDA. Wrong answer. The Provos are big in this area. My daddy's a big fella in the Provos, so when the son gets out after five years inside, guess who's the young pretender? Meanwhile, she still writes her twenty-two page letters to him every night and has done since the beginning. Not that he's worth it, but you have to admire her tenacity for sticking with him. That's the only loyalty I know or care about. Loyalty to someone you love, regardless! I'd like to think if I loved someone I'd follow that person to hell! Politics has nothing to do with it!

JOSIE. One day you will understand, when you come to the

limits of what you can do by yourself, that this is not dogma, that there are no personal differences between one person and another that are not political.

FRIEDA.   You can't believe that.

JOSIE.   I do. I do.

DONNA.   I wish you two would give over. You're like chalk and cheese, you always have been.

JOSIE.   Do you know what they did when they divided this country —

FRIEDA.   Oh, here we go again. Mystical alienation.

JOSIE.   They gave us political amnesia.

FRIEDA.   Jargon.

DONNA.   *(Getting up.)* Would anyone like a drink? I'm going to open a bottle.

FRIEDA.   Do you mean to tell me you've got booze in this house?

DONNA.   Did you get me any sugar?

FRIEDA.   *(Waves her hand.)* Oh, apart from the Château Lenadoon.

DONNA.   *(Hurt.)* What's wrong with it?

FRIEDA.   I think the French do it better.

DONNA.   Do you not want any?

FRIEDA.   I will if there's nothing else.

DONNA.   Will you have a drink, Josie? It'll relax you?

JOSIE.   I shouldn't.

DONNA.   *(Disappearing to the kitchen.)* I'll bring three glasses.

FRIEDA.   When does Liam actually get out?

JOSIE.   Two weeks.

FRIEDA.   What will you do? Stay on here?

JOSIE.   No. Probably move back to my daddy's.

FRIEDA.   After all this time? You'll enjoy that.

JOSIE.   I don't see any alternative.

FRIEDA.   I'm glad it's not me. I wouldn't want to be his house-keeper.

JOSIE.   It's purely economic.

FRIEDA.   Oh, now. We never do anything we don't want to do.

JOSIE.   But we do! Often.

DONNA.   *(Returning.)* It looks a bit cloudy, but I expect it'll

19

settle.

FRIEDA.   When do you want me to do your hair?

DONNA.   I've changed my mind.

FRIEDA.   Why?

DONNA.   If I go up to the prison tomorrow with dyed hair Liam'll think I'm running after somebody.

FRIEDA.   So what?

DONNA.   So it's not worth the fights.

FRIEDA.   That's ridiculous. *(Doorbell.)*

JOSIE.   Who's that at this time? *(Donna moves cautiously to look out of the window. She turns out the light and pulls back the curtain, rattling the venetian blind as she looks out without being seen from the outside.)*

DONNA.   It's two men. Jesus Christ! It's your daddy! *(She switches the light on again. Josie lifts the bottle and glasses and runs into the kitchen. Frieda does not move. The doorbell rings again as Josie returns.)* What'll I do?

JOSIE.   Wait a minute. *(To Frieda.)* Get rid of that ashtray! And open the back door.

FRIEDA.   *(Unmoved.)* What for?

JOSIE.   To let fresh air in.

FRIEDA.   The whole place stinks. He'll know. *(Doorbell, more urgently.)*

JOSIE.   *(To Donna.)* All right, open it. *(Donna exits to open the front door. Josie rushes into the kitchen with the three glasses and the bottle of wine, while Frieda refuses to cooperate.)*

FRIEDA.   What are you tidying up for? Why don't you be yourself? *(Donna lets two men quickly into the room. One of them is Malachy McCoy, Josie's and Frieda's father. The other is a younger man whom the women have never seen before.)*

MALACHY.   *(Reacting to the smoke-filled room; he waves his arm in front of his face.)* In the name a'Jesus! Is this how you spend your time? Who's been smoking in here?

FRIEDA.   I have!

MALACHY.   Oh yes. *(Coughing violently.)* It would be you. You think because you're living round at your auntie's you can do what you like. I'll bring you home one of these days if you're not careful.

FRIEDA. Suits me. I wouldn't have to look after them.

MALACHY. What have you got on your head?

FRIEDA. Tinfoil.

MALACHY. I can see that! *(Josie returns, he puts his arm round her to draw her near in a bear hug.)* How's my mate! Hey!

JOSIE. *(Resisting the embrace.)* I'm not your mate. I'm your daughter.

MALACHY. *(Angry, releasing her from his grip.)* Jesus Christ! What's wrong with you, for God's sake!

FRIEDA. *(Sweetly, to Joe.)* Don't mind our father. It's just that we don't have a mother any more and he's kinda protective.

MALACHY. That's enough from you.

FRIEDA. Well, are you going to introduce us or do we have to do it ourselves?

MALACHY. This is Joe Conran.

JOE. Hello.

MALACHY. My daughter, Josie.

JOSIE. Hello.

MALACHY. *(Coughs.)* This is Donna, my son's wife.

DONNA. Hello Joe.

MALACHY. And that creature in the tinfoil — for whatever reason — is my other daughter, Frieda.

FRIEDA. Hello Joe Conran.

MALACHY. Joe's going to stop here for a while. Maybe a couple of nights or so.

JOSIE. I wasn't expecting you.

MALACHY. We weren't expecting to be raided at the top end of the estate.

JOSIE. Oh, I see.

MALACHY. Did you not hear them?

JOSIE. Yes, earlier.

MALACHY. What a night. I don't know where they're getting their information from. This is probably the safest place. He's in your care — from now on.

JOSIE. I see.

MALACHY. *(To Donna and Frieda.)* You're not to go asking him any questions about what he's doing here. Do you hear me, Frieda? *(She feigns surprise. To Joe.)* And you're not to answer any

21

questions until the time comes. She's a mouth like the QE2. Josie's responsible for you.

JOE. Fine.

DONNA. Where's he going to sleep?

MALACHY. He can sleep down here on the sofa. Sure, it's only for an odd night.

JOSIE. No, he can't do that. He can have my bed. *(Frieda is looking wide-eyed at Josie. Josie ignores her.)* He probably needs his sleep. I'll sleep down here.

JOE. Oh, no, I couldn't — I'm used to sleeping — anywhere — and this is very nice. I couldn't put you out.

JOSIE. You're not putting me out.

MALACHY. Well, sort it out between you. I'll be on my way. *(To Josie, taking her aside.)* You know what your instructions are. *(Josie nods.)* Liam will be out soon ... you'll be coming home ... I'll get your room painted.

JOSIE. We'll see.

MALACHY. I'll be glad to have him back — the business is too much for one.

DONNA. Sure I thought Gabriel was helping you.

MALACHY. Gabriel nearly ruined me. He paints everything that moves. A woman rang me up the other day — he'd painted all her windows shut. Nobody paints gloss like Liam.

DONNA. Would you like a cup of tea before you go?

MALACHY. No thanks, I'd better be getting back. *(He turns to go.)*

FRIEDA. Daddy! Will you be at the Prisoners' Dependents "do?"

MALACHY. Why?

FRIEDA. I'm singing one of my own compositions.

MALACHY. I don't know. I'll see. Wait a minute. *(Puts his hand into his pocket.)* Here's a couple of quid. Buy yourselves a bar of chocolate.

JOSIE. Thanks, Daddy.

DONNA. Cheerio, Mr. McCoy.

FRIEDA. Good-bye, Father. *(Malachy exits.)* Chocolates! Sweeties! What age does he think we are! A bottle of whiskey would be more like it.

JOE.   I have one in my travelling bag. I got it on the boat. *(He puts his bag on the floor.)*

FRIEDA.   *(Full of admiration.)* Good man!

JOSIE.   *(Restraining Joe from opening his bag.)* I suggest you keep it in your bag. My sister and a glass of whiskey are quite a combination.

FRIEDA.   Am I? That's the nicest thing you've said about me all evening.

JOSIE.   The grain and the grape don't mix. Your wine's in the kitchen.

DONNA.   *(To Joe.)* Would you like a cuppa tea, Joe?

JOE.   I don't drink tea.

DONNA.   You're joking.

JOE.   No, I'm not.

DONNA.   Coffee?

JOE.   Yes, that would be lovely.

DONNA.   Right.

FRIEDA.   Why do you not drink tea?

DONNA.   Frieda!

FRIEDA.   No, I'm interested. Do you not like it?

JOE.   No.

FRIEDA.   Did something happen to put you off it?

JOE.   When I was at school I had to drink tea and I didn't like it, so I've never drunk it since.

FRIEDA.   When you were at school?

DONNA.   Was that like a boarding school?

JOE.   Public school, yes.

FRIEDA.   What public school did you go to?

JOE.   I went to Eton. *(Donna and Frieda can hardly suppress their disbelief. Only Josie appears uninterested and even impatient.)*

DONNA.   Well, if you'll excuse me for a minute I'll just get you a cup of coffee. *(She exits. Frieda sits down beside Joe.)*

JOSIE.   Your wine's in the kitchen.

FRIEDA.   Donna'll bring it out when she's coming.

JOSIE.   We've got some homemade wine, would you like some?

JOE.   No, thank you.

FRIEDA.   You don't like wine either?

JOE. No, I do, very much. But I prefer to leave it to the experts.

FRIEDA. That's just what I said.

JOE. Would you like a cigarette, Frieda? You smoke, don't you?

FRIEDA. Listen, we all do, but these two are so afraid of my da they won't admit it.

JOE. *(Laughs.)* Oh, I see. Well, help yourselves. *(They take the packet.)* Do you live here as well?

FRIEDA. No, I live round the corner.

JOE. You're a singer?

FRIEDA. You've heard about me?

JOE. You told your father you were singing one of your own compositions.

FRIEDA. I'm a singer/songwriter.

JOSIE. She works in the hairdresser's by the bus depot.

FRIEDA. I still sing.

DONNA. *(Opening the kitchen door.)* Do you like it made with milk or water?

JOE. I like it black, thanks.

DONNA. *(To herself.)* Black. *(Withdrawing again.)*

JOE. Is that what you want to be, a professional singer?

FRIEDA. Och, no — that's only a front. What I really want is to marry somebody rich and live abroad.

JOE. I'm not exactly sure when you're serious and when you're joking.

FRIEDA. Oh, I'm perfectly serious. Do you think I want to end up like my big sister here? Running about like a wee messenger girl for my father and his cronies. No thanks. And if she's not careful she'll finish up like my auntie Cora. Do you know about my father's maiden sisters?

JOE. No.

FRIEDA. I live with them. Cora is blind and deaf and dumb and she has no hands, and she's been like that since she was eighteen. And Bridget, the other one, is a maid because she stayed to look after Cora. And I'm still a maid because I'm looking after both of them.

JOE. What happened to your aunt when she was eighteen?

FRIEDA. Oh, the usual. She was storing ammunition for her wee brother Malachy — my father, God love him — who was in the IRA even then. He asked her to move it. Unfortunately it was in poor condition, technically what you call weeping. So when she pulled up the floorboards in her bedroom whoosh! It took the skin off her face. Her hair's never really grown properly since and look — no hands! *(She demonstrates by pulling her fists up into her sleeves. Donna comes into the room with coffee for Joe.)*

DONNA. God forgive you! *(To Joe.)* I hope this is all right.

FRIEDA. They stick her out at the front of the parades every so often to show the women of Ireland what their patriotic duty should be. But I'll tell you something — it won't be mine!

JOSIE. She was supposed to have been a beautiful girl, my auntie Cora. My father told me that. So I suppose you could say she really had something to sacrifice.

DONNA. We've all got something to sacrifice!

FRIEDA. You're right! And when there's a tricolour over the City Hall, Donna will still be making coffee for Joe Conran, and Josie will still be keeping house for her daddy, because it doesn't matter a damn whether the British are here or not.

JOSIE. That's just your excuse for not doing anything.

FRIEDA. Aye. But it's a good one. *(To Joe.)* So, Joe Conran, now that you know about us, what are you doing here?

JOE. *(Looking to Josie, who gives him no help whatsoever.)* I'm not supposed to answer any questions.

FRIEDA. Oh come on, this is family.

JOE. My grandfather was Irish. He married a Catholic. My grandmother, Teresa Conran, was a friend of Connolly's.

DONNA. James Connolly?

FRIEDA. You're here because your granny knew Connolly? *(Pause.)* She didn't meet him at the parents' association at Eton, did she?

JOSIE. Frieda?

FRIEDA. What?

JOSIE. How long did you say you had to keep the tinfoil on for?

FRIEDA. *(Touches her head.)* Oh fuck! Ten minutes! *(Dashes out and slams the door.)*

DONNA. I think I'd better help her with the head dress. *(She exits.)*

JOE. So you're the courier? *(Josie nods.)* What exactly do you do?

JOSIE. I take messages between the commanders, move the stuff from one place to another, or people. I operate at nights mostly, which is why I was offering you my bed. I'm hardly ever in it.

JOE. Your security's not very good on this estate. I'd only just arrived when the Army came up the road. Why did that happen?

JOSIE. There've been a lot of raids recently. Informers using the confidential telephones — it's always the same after a bombing campaign.

JOE. Are the others involved? *(Indicates the kitchen.)*

JOSIE. Donna has a child to look after.

JOE. And Frieda?

JOSIE. Well, you've seen her.

JOE. Can they be trusted?

JOSIE. This is family.

JOE. You must be very brave.

JOSIE. I'm not brave. I just began doing this before I had to think of the consequences. I think I'm more scared than I was ten years ago. But I'm getting better at smiling at soldiers. *(She smiles at him.)*

JOE. You shouldn't do that.

JOSIE. What?

JOE. Smile at soldiers.

JOSIE. Why not?

JOE. If you smile to deceive, how will I know when it's for real?

JOSIE. *(Laughs.)* I think that's the least of your worries.

JOE. Worries? Do I have worries?

JOSIE. Now humour I didn't expect.

JOE. What did you expect? *(She gets up.)*

JOSIE. I have to go out for a while.

JOE. Are you married, Josie?

JOSIE. *(Putting on her coat.)* No.

JOE. Do you have a boyfriend?

JOSIE. You ask too many questions, Joe Conran.

JOE. I know, but you have such beautiful eyes I can't help wondering.

JOSIE. I'm very puritanical. I wanted to be a nun once — and you're not going to charm your way into this organization.

JOE. Charm? I was interrogated in Amsterdam!

JOSIE. You weren't interrogated, you were questioned. There are still some questions you need to answer before we're satisfied.

JOE. But how long, how long am I going to be here?

JOSIE. For a while.

JOE. So I'm not going to meet anyone tonight?

JOSIE. No. You're going to stay here with me for a while. *(Frieda's voice offstage from the kitchen, singing: "Oh love is pleasing and love is teasing and love is —")* I suggest you go to bed soon. Then you won't have to tell any more lies. Eton? You surprise me. *(Josie exits by the front door. Joe sits down. The singing stops as Frieda enters the room carrying a glass in each hand. She has a towel around her head like a turban and she is dressed only in a long towelling dressing-gown, which is tied at the waist. Joe pays no attention to her entrance until she speaks.)*

FRIEDA. I'm sorry I was so long. *(She puts the empty glasses down, and begins to rummage through Joe's travelling bag.)*

JOE. What are you doing?

FRIEDA. You said you had whiskey. I'm looking for it. *(She takes the bottle out.)* Would you like a glass?

JOE. Thanks. *(She pours whiskey.)*

FRIEDA. Would you have a cigarette?

JOE. I think you have the packet.

FRIEDA. Oh, so I have. *(She sits down on the sofa beside him. Joe remains obstinately preoccupied, and looking around the room.)*

JOE. I wanted to ask you something.

FRIEDA. Yes?

JOE. Why are you so critical of your family's involvement with the Republican movement?

27

FRIEDA. Oh, I wouldn't say I was critical exactly. I mean, I respect them all very much. My father's a great man and Josie's so committed. You have to admire her and Liam's dedication. I mean, what the Brits have done to my family would make you weep.

JOE. But you're not an activist?

FRIEDA. No. Well, I used to be. I gave all that up in the seventies. God, I was on more demonstrations than enough.

JOE. So you're not political at all now?

FRIEDA. Well, that's not true either. I sing.

JOE. You sing?

FRIEDA. Yes. That's what I do instead. *(She gets up as she is speaking and walks around the room, finally turning to face him.)* Can you see my pubic hair?

JOE. No.

FRIEDA. Oh good. I was a bit worried in case you could. I'm anti-nationalist, that's all.

JOE. What do you mean by that?

FRIEDA. Nationalism is always the last resort of people who've failed to achieve anything else. Joe, could we be friends? *(Sits down beside him again, very close.)*

JOE. Well, I wouldn't want to argue with you, Frieda.

FRIEDA. Oh, but I love arguing. Before Donna comes in, there's something I've been wanting to tell you — you're disturbing me and I'd like to do something about it. Since you walked in here tonight I thought — yes, him! Let me see your hand. *(She grabs his hand.)* Are you a Scorpio?

JOE. I'm very easily seduced. I'm on a job here — I don't want to get involved. *(Donna comes in from the kitchen. She has a towel over her shoulders, she has just washed her hair.)*

DONNA. I see you've opened the whiskey, Frieda. *(Joe gets up.)*

JOE. Can you tell me where you want me to sleep?

DONNA. Oh yes, of course. I'm sorry. I should have said so earlier. Josie's room at the top of the stairs.

JOE. Thank you. Good night.

DONNA. What about your whiskey?

JOE. Please help yourselves. Good night. *(He leaves the room.*

Footsteps heard on the stairs.)

DONNA. Do you have to throw yourself at every man on the run who stays under my roof! What do you think this place is?

FRIEDA. What's wrong, did I get to him first?

DONNA. You watch your tongue!

FRIEDA. You never object to Josie doing it. She threw herself at him as soon as he arrived. He's sleeping in her bed for God's sake. Don't think I don't know why Josie stays here, and not at home with my father. Helping you with Catherine. My God, I've never seen any evidence of it.

DONNA. Josie, whatever she does, is older than you are.

FRIEDA. Josie's older than any of us.

DONNA. That may well be …

FRIEDA. At least four hundred years! *(Freida begins to cry.)*

DONNA. You shouldn't drink. Whiskey always makes you cry.

FRIEDA. Nobody seems to care what happens to me. If I died tomorrow — it would be no loss.

DONNA. I care, Frieda.

FRIEDA. Oh yes, I know, but I was talking about love!

DONNA. I love you, Frieda.

FRIEDA. Yes, I know, but I want to be happy with someone! I haven't anyone of my own. Sometimes when I'm walking along the street and I see a couple holding hands I have to look away — I'm so jealous. Other times I look closely at the woman and think, well, I'm more attractive than her, why doesn't that man notice me? And lots of times I just wander around looking at men.

DONNA. Happiness requires all your intelligence. You won't find it just by looking; and the only thing you'll get from a man who looks like Joe Conran is a lot of trouble. But that's only my opinion. You must make up your own mind.

FRIEDA. *(Sniffing.)* No. It's all right. I don't fancy him, anyway. I think he's got sexual problems.

DONNA. *(Putting the top on the whiskey bottle.)* Oh well, that's all right then. Let's have a look at this hair of yours and see how well it's taken.

FRIEDA. No, wait. I have to dry it first. *(Frieda exits.)*

Scene 3

Donna, Josie.

Several hours later. Donna is in bed. A cot stands beside the bed and a night light by the cot. Slowly the door opens in the dark and light falls across the room. A figure is silhouetted in the doorway; the figure aproaches the cot. Donna turns instinctively as the figure approaches.

DONNA.   Who's there? *(The baby murmurs.)* Please don't wake her.

JOSIE.   It's all right, she's looking for us.

DONNA.   What did you say?

JOSIE.   She's looking through her life for us. She'll be back in a minute. *(Donna gets out of bed quickly and takes Josie's arm.)*

DONNA.   Wake up, Josie. Wake up.

JOSIE.   Oh. Oh. *(Shivering.)* I'm very cold.

DONNA.   Come to bed. *(Donna helps her into bed.)* Here, I'll make a bucket with my nightdress. It's better than the sofa ... Do you remember when we were kids we used to do this. You, me and Frieda in a double bed. We all had to face in the same direction or we wouldn't fit in. Except Frieda kept turning the other way and we had to push her out. She'd run off crying to your mammy and we'd to bribe her to keep her quiet ... What's wrong? Was he not at the meeting?

JOSIE.   He knew I was going to be there, but he didn't wait!

DONNA.   You're shivering, hold on to me.

JOSIE.   He left before I arrived, Donna. Half an hour. He's in this town, he talked to Frieda tonight, but he wouldn't wait for me!

DONNA.   Don't abandon yourself like this!

JOSIE.   He told me I invaded his life.

DONNA.   Invaded. It's not a word I would use.

JOSIE.   Oh, Donna, I did make him happy. I did!

DONNA.   I know, love. I know.

Scene 4

Frieda, Danny, McDermot, Malachy, Gabriel, Second Man.

*Frieda is sitting on a high stool in a circle of light. The set-
ting is the Club. Hanging down from the walls behind her are
portraits of the ten dead hungry strikers, visible now that the
lights are on. Frieda's song is accompanied by Danny at the
piano.*

FRIEDA.

> When I was young my father
> Walked me through the hall to see
> Where Connolly, Pearse and Plunkett hung;
> A profile against the darkening sky
> My father pointed out to me,
> Was the greatest name of all,
> To be called the Volunteer,
> To be called the Volunteer.
>
> When I grew up my first love
> Whispered in my ear,
> What do you most desire, my love?
> What do you most desire?
> Lying on a moonlit beach
> I held his hand and said
> To be a Volunteer, my love,
> To be a Volunteer.

*(Someone is whistling. Danny stops, addressing a young man in the
darkness.)*

DANNY.   I'm sorry, you can't come in. We're not open till
seven. This is a rehearsal.

McDERMOT.   It's not a rehearsal she needs; it's an education!

FRIEDA.   *(Covering her eyes from the lights and peering out into the
darkness.)* Who is that?

McDERMOT.   I came to see what you did in your spare time.

31

FRIEDA. John McDermot, have you gone mad!
DANNY. Do you know him?
FRIEDA. Could we take a break now?
McDERMOT. Come back in a hundred years; she needs all the time she can get!
FRIEDA. Go on. *(Pushing the hesitant Danny out.)* It's all right. He really is a friend of mine. *(Danny exits.)* Why do your jokes always sound like a threat?
McDERMOT. You think I was joking?
FRIEDA. What are you doing here anyway?
McDERMOT. You were supposed to be selling papers with me on Saturday. What happened to you?
FRIEDA. You're mad coming in here!
McDERMOT. What did you do to your hair? Is that a disguise so I wouldn't ever recognize you again
FRIEDA. Oh, don't you start.
McDERMOT. On second thoughts, it's just as well you didn't come out on Saturday. I would have had to explain that your appearance was your own idea and in no way rejected the views of the Workers' Party.
FRIEDA. It's for my act.
McDERMOT. The song you were singing, was that part of your act as well?
FRIEDA. Before you say anything devastating, I wrote that song.
McDERMOT. I thought you did. *(Pause.)* Do you want to know what I think?
FRIEDA. *(Puts her hands over her ears.)* I don't want to hear. I never listen to criticism. *(Frieda has her hands over her ears and she is humming. He pulls her hands away.)*
McDERMOT. Listen, you! It's about time you came out of the closet and stood up for what you believe in. Instead of singing these endless Republican dirges around the clubs! "The greatest name of all, to be a Volunteer!"
FRIEDA. I wrote it after Bobby Sands died. It's very popular here, you know. It's always requested.
McDERMOT. Listen, kid. You want to be big? You want to lead

the tribe, not follow it. This song celebrates militarism. How many times have you been told it's the Party not the Army that is dominant. The political thinker, not the soldier. That's the greatest name of all. You know that — you've known it since you were seventeen. You must use everything you know when you write songs, Frieda.

FRIEDA. There haven't been many moments in my life when I've felt honest; the feeling I had when I wrote that song was one of them. When I feel I can write a song about the Party I'll let you know.

McDERMOT. He who suffers the most! That's you all over. You weep at Bobby Sands's funeral, but a bomb in a store and the IRA are bastards. You could end up on both sides of the border if you don't think!

FRIEDA. At least I'd see everybody's point of view.

McDERMOT. If you can see everybody's point of view you can see nothing at all. What you lack is a conceptual framework.

FRIEDA. One of these days, John McDermot, you'll collapse in a conceptual framework. *(A door bangs. Gabriel appears.)*

GABRIEL. You're a bit out of your territory, fella.

McDERMOT. And you're out of your depth — son.

FRIEDA. Look, Gabriel, we don't want any trouble. He's with me. We were just leaving.

GABRIEL. My uncle Malachy won't like it when he hears about this.

FRIEDA. He can say what he likes, I've never been afraid of my father. I'm not about to start because he's drilling the Boy Scouts!

GABRIEL. You can tell him that yourself. *(Door bangs.)* Here he is now. *(Malachy comes in, followed by the Second Man.)*

FRIEDA. Oh fuck! *(Frieda takes John's arm and braces herself to confront Malachy.)*

MALACHY. What's he doing here?

FRIEDA. He's with me.

MALACHY. Get him out of here!

FRIEDA. No, no. Wait! *(McDermot and Frieda are dragged apart.)*

SECOND MAN. Have you no control over your daughter?

(McDermot is pushed roughly towards the door by Gabriel and the Second Man. They exit. Malachy has caught Frieda by the wrist to restrain her from following. He now pushes her across the room.)

MALACHY. You stay — *(Frieda is struck on the back of the head by Malachy.)* — away from him! *(Frieda remains holding her head, momentarily stunned.)* You'll not make a little boy of me! I'm sick to death of hearing about you … All I get is complaints … bringing that hood in here.

FRIEDA. *(Recovering.)* What do I have to do or say, Father, to get you to leave me alone —

MALACHY. I'll leave you alone all right. I'll leave you so you'll wish you'd never been born. *(He makes a race at her. She pushes a table into his path.)*

FRIEDA. Oh, Mammy. Mammy. *(He attempts to punch her in the stomach.)*

MALACHY. You'll not make little of me. Siding with the people who condemned Bobby Sands.

FRIEDA. *(Backing away towards the door.)* They didn't condemn him. They said he beat his wife! Hard to believe, isn't it?

MALACHY. Get out of my sight. *(Overturned club furniture stands between them.)*

FRIEDA. They say when he was dying she was so afraid of him she wouldn't go up to the prison to see him. In fact she wouldn't go near him until she was sure he was definitely dead.

MALACHY. Never let me see your face again.

FRIEDA. *(Still backing out.)* You know something, Father? You've been burying your friends since 'sixty-nine. But do you know something else, your friends have been burying you!

MALACHY. Never cross my door again!

FRIEDA. *(Desperation.)* We are the dying. Why are we mourning them! *(She points at the portraits of the dead hunger strikers. She exits.)*

Scene 5

Danny, Gabriel, Second Man, McDermot, Frieda.

Outside the Club, at the back, John McDermot is on the ground trying to protect his ribs and head from the feet of his two attackers.

Danny comes rushing in on them.

DANNY.   For Christ's sake, are you mad?

GABRIEL.   What's wrong with you, McLoughlin!

DANNY.   There's a foot patrol at the top of the entry — you can hear yous a mile away.

GABRIEL.   Beat it! *(The two men run off, Danny appears to follow, then stops and returns to McDermot.)*

DANNY.   Are you OK?

McDERMOT.   *(Beginning to look for his glasses.)* I don't know yet. I can't see a thing.

DANNY.   *(Stoops to retrieve them.)* I'm afraid they're broken.

McDERMOT.   *(Taking them from him.)* Oh shit. I have another pair but — they're not as good. *(He tries to fix them.)* I hope I can remember where I put them.

DANNY.   I don't know who you are or where you're coming from but next time they'll kill you ... *(McDermot doesn't reply.)* Is she worth it?

McDERMOT.   Did you say the Army were about?

DANNY.   Aye, for their benefit. *(Frieda's footsteps are heard coming towards them.)*

FRIEDA.   Where's John McDermot?

DANNY.   Hey, Frieda! Over here! He's OK, calm down! He'll live.

FRIEDA.   *(Gets down on her knees to face John, who is propped against the wall.)* You stupid, thoughtless, reckless, insensitive, selfish bastard!

DANNY.   Aye, well, I'll head away on.

35

FRIEDA. I could murder you! You have blown my one chance! Walking in there tonight and brazenly exhibiting yourself.
DANNY. I wouldn't hang about. Those boys might come back.
(Danny exits.)
McDERMOT. You didn't have to say you were with me.
FRIEDA. Who did you come to talk to — my daddy?
McDERMOT. I'm sorry.
FRIEDA. *(Getting to her feet.)* Well, you're responsible for me now.
McDERMOT. Don't be silly. Nobody's responsible for you ... Are you all right?
FRIEDA. No, I'm not. My head aches and my stomach's heaving — I think I'm going to be sick.
McDERMOT. It's the shock!
FRIEDA. Shock? My life's in ruins. My father thinks I'm in the Workers' Party, and he thinks you and I are lovers. Jesus, when our Liam gets out of the Kesh he'll probably kill both of us.
McDERMOT. What do you want to do about it?
FRIEDA. I've made a decision.
McDERMOT. What's that?
FRIEDA. I'd like to join the Party.
McDERMOT. That's a step in the right direction.
FRIEDA. It's a beginning.
McDERMOT. Why?
FRIEDA. I have never in my life forgiven anyone who raised their hand to me.
McDERMOT. I'll try to remember.
FRIEDA. I have another problem. I'm homeless and I don't have any money. Do you think you could find me somewhere to live?
McDERMOT. I could take in a lodger.
FRIEDA. This is serious.
McDERMOT. I am serious.
FRIEDA. Would your wife not mind?
McDERMOT. We separated six months ago.
FRIEDA. In that case, no, I think not. Surely some other member of the Party could help me.
McDERMOT. There's someone who visits me from time to

36

time. Between you and me would be a business arrangement. I'm hardly ever at home.

FRIEDA.   All right. I accept. The other thing is — I really don't have any money at the moment. I packed in my job at the hairdresser's.

McDERMOT.   I think that was wise.

FRIEDA.   I want to devote more time to writing songs.

McDERMOT.   Well, I wouldn't depend on making a living from your singing career just yet, Frieda.

FRIEDA.   You think not

McDERMOT.   Your material isn't very commercial.

FRIEDA.   I'm trying to get a gig at the Orpheus — or somewhere.

McDERMOT.   Well, I can't do anything about that — but we can come to some arrangement about the money when you've got some. *(Begins to try to struggle to his feet.)* Now, would you like to help me up from here. My back's killing me.

FRIEDA.   *(Helping him with her arm.)* Why are you doing this?

McDERMOT.   *(In some pain.)* Because someone put his boot in my rib cage.

FRIEDA.   No. Why are you helping me?

McDERMOT.   Because you're lost, Frieda. You're lost and I'm half blind.

FRIEDA.   *(Going off with him.)* I'm not lost! I just don't want all those people on my side. Do you?

Scene 6

Joe, Josie, O'Donnell, Malachy.

The Club. In addition to the portraits of the hunger strikers there are balloons and decorations around the room. It is after closing time and the chairs are upturned on the table tops. Joe follows Josie into the room. She switches on a small light above a table and lifts down two chairs, standing them upright on the floor.

37

JOE. *(Looking around.)* This is very festive.

JOSIE.   It's our Club. My brother's getting out tomorrow and there's to be a party.

JOE.   How long's he been away?

JOSIE.   Five years.

JOE.   The baby's nearly two?

JOSIE.   Parole. He gets out on parole.

JOE.   And in between she waits?

JOSIE.   Of course she waits.

JOE.   When was the last time he was out?

JOSIE.   He was at the birth.

JOE.   Would you wait two years for a man, Josie?

JOSIE.   For the right man.

JOE.   Are you waiting for the right man?

JOSIE.   Sit down.

JOE.   You seem nervous.

JOSIE.   It's cold in here.

JOE.   When do I get to meet O'Donnell?

JOSIE.   When you've answered my questions.

JOE.   Your questions?

JOSIE.   A lot of people want to meet O'Donnell, Joe. The British don't even know what he looks like. We know that.

JOE.   All right, but this is the third time I will have been questioned. Amsterdam, Dublin, and now here.

JOSIE.   I promise you this will be the last. *(Joe sits in the chair Josie has indicated. Taking a file from her shoulder bag and placing it on the table she also sits down.)* I saw this report on you — I've been dying to meet you since I read it. *(Reads from the file.)* Educated Trinity and Cambridge. First class honours Sociology. Ph.D. Chairman of the Socialist Society. Revolutionary Socialist Students' Federation. Member of the European International Liberation Group ... ardent supporter of the Basque Separatist Movement ... recently brought a group of left-wing German students into talks with the Free Wales Army on anti-technology in industry, or how to prevent, by force if necessary, the replacement of workers by machines. Also set up discussions between the Italian Communist-controlled administrations of several states and the British Left — including some of

38

our people in Britain — on advantages of the local state. Items on the agenda: the control of police, Army and security systems, also the subsidization of communes. You're a clever fellow. Oh, and something else. You've got a very interesting emotional life. Married: 1971. Several girlfriends. Currently: in Spain, a Basque lawyer; in Germany, Hamburg, a Marxist psychoanalyst; in Italy, a dancer, or was it an actress with a socialist theatre company, whose father is a mayor of a Communist town. Now, after all those exotic locations, what brings you to West Belfast?

JOE. You make me sound like a tourist. I do take my politics home with me. *(Pause.)* My wife's an Irish Catholic.

JOSIE. I wouldn't cite loyalty to your wife as a reason for your being here — it's not exactly your most stable characteristic.

JOE. We have an arrangement.

JOSIE. That's very nice. But it doesn't answer my question.

JOE. What exactly do you want to know?

JOSIE. Let me tell you a story, Joe. When I was little my daddy used to say — "When the British withdraw we can be human." I believed that, since the south of Ireland was already free, there I could be human … Well, I'd been down south quite a few times, always to Bodenstown to the Wolfe Tone Commemorations and that meant coming back on the coach again as soon as it was over. One year when I was nearly sixteen, instead of coming straight back I stayed on and went to Dublin. I simply wanted to see the capital … I had no money and my shoes let in water, and I came back to Belfast at night with very wet feet in the back of a pig lorry. I smelt of pig feed. It dropped me off at seven-thirty in the morning on the Falls Road. I had time to go home and change before going to school at nine … There was a girl next to me in assembly. She had long straight fair hair and gleaming white teeth. If you leaned close she smelt of lemon soap. When she went to Dublin it was to buy clothes, she told me. I stood looking down at her beautifully polished shoes and I knew that it was all for her. Dublin existed for her to buy her shoes in … All day the smell of pig feed stayed with me … From then on I stopped wanting only British withdrawal — to unite Ireland for the shoppers and the shopkeepers of Belfast and Dublin. I became a revolutionary. You see it wasn't the presence of the British that made me feel unclean that morning — it was the presence of money — Irish money as much as English money. Do you understand, Joe? What I want to know is, what are you doing in the ranks of the unhuman? I was born here. *(Joe thinks for a minute, then reaches into his pocket, takes out his wallet, from which he quickly takes all the notes, and thrusts both wallet and notes into Josie's hands.)*

JOE.   Buy them! ... Buy shoes! ... You're not a revolutionary, Josie, you're a shoe fetishist. Go out, fill yourself with all the things that make you envious, then when you've got it out of your system — come back and talk to me seriously about revolution ... You want to know what I'm doing here? It's very simple: I'm taking responsibility for what is made of me.

JOSIE.   *(Puts the wallet and the money back on the table between them.)* What is made of you?

JOE.   Ascendancy. Anglo-Irish. British Army. I was born there. A prisoner of circumstances you might say; circumstances which found me enrolling in Sandhurst when I was seventeen, before I could think. But I did think — so I changed. I stopped being a soldier. And I've continued to resist circumstances ever since.

JOSIE.   Would you die for an impossibility?

JOE.   No ... I don't think so ... What impossibility?

JOSIE.   The thirty-two-county Workers' Republic. Connolly's dream. Some of our people, and I'm one of them, believe it to be an impossibility. A place we will never come into. But we'll die trying to get there, because I suppose this is our country and as it is our lives are meaningless ... But your life isn't meaningless, Joe, with your international conferences and your international girl friends ... It's hard to imagine a better life. So, come on, why are you risking so much for us? And this isn't even your country?

JOE.   Not for you — for the revolution. I happen to be one of those people who believe that my government's aggression in another country has something to do with me. I also know full well that there cannot be an English revolution unless there is one in Ireland. "A nation that enslaves another ..."

40

JOSIE. "... can never itself be free." You'll find that slogan on the wall behind the swimming baths. We've come a long way. Ten years ago we wouldn't have dared quote Marx on the gable walls. Now we simply don't bother to attribute it to him ... But what would make you, with your background, support a revolution? You've too much to lose.

JOE. Absolutely. I have too much to lose. You have to trust my integrity. You put too much emphasis on the weight of experience — I am the sum of all my reading.

JOSIE. Of your reading? Do you mean books? Jesus ... Your fucking ideas, Joe. I'm trying to find out how you actually feel. The thing is — why would you be a traitor to your own country?

JOE. I'm not a traitor — my father was an Irish Protestant son of a mixed marriage. My grandparents were Southern Unionists. My mother is an English Catholic. I was sent to Ampleforth. I went into the Army as an engineer — yes. My mother's family are all British Army. I left the Army after eighteen months and have had no connections with it since. I went back to university and read sociology and became a believer in revolutionary socialism.

JOSIE. Like many other sons of the bourgeoisie in the sixties. Fascinating generation. God I hated them. Made it all too clear to you who was in and who was out. I imagine you were in, Joe.

JOE. You seem to object to the idea that a person can refuse to render back what their social conditioning will make of them. And yet the history of the world we live in, of change and revolution, suggests we do just that very thing.

JOSIE. I'm objecting to the fact that you refuse to talk about your emotional involvement with the British.

JOE. The question of identity is very complex.

JOSIE. So it is, Joe. *(She waits while he appears to think.)* In fact it's crucial. *(Very quietly, while still awaiting his reply.)* We've had a number of volunteers who come to us, usually Catholics married to Protestants, driven out of an area by loyalist intimidation. They get bitter about it and join the Republican movement to hit back. They're the worst type of volunteers as far as I'm concerned. They hit back because all they wanted was to be good Protestants, to be acceptable, like the working class who want to be middle class; blacks who want to be white. This type of volunteer hates the Protestants and the British because they are not Protestant and they are not British. They are not entirely trustworthy either because they will be among the first to back the state should conditions improve; and they will never make good revolutionaries because they are not fighting to be what they are. Until we know what you are; until you know who you are, how can we trust your motives for being here?

JOE.   I didn't realize the Republican Movement was so choosy about the conscience of its recruits!

JOSIE.   It's a bit like the Catholic Church, Joe; easy if you were born in it, difficult if you try to convert.

JOE.   I regard myself as Irish!

JOSIE.   There's no need to go that far. The thing is — are you rejecting Mother because Mother's rejecting you?

JOE.   This is extraordinary.

JOSIE.   You're no ordinary recruit, Joe. And it really doesn't concern us whether you regard yourself as Irish or English. You have already met on your travels a number of English socialists who work for us. If we hesitate it has nothing to do with your nationality; it is merely because we have very strong doubts about your motives.

JOE.   You've said that before. What doubts?

JOSIE.   Your family?

JOE.   My wife's an Irish Catholic.

JOSIE.   I was talking about a more binding relationship than that one — your mother's a hard woman to impress, I imagine. Was she impressed by your marriage to Rosa Connelly?

JOE.   My mother's not important to me. I hardly ever see her.

JOSIE.   Is that right?

JOE.   She's retired to South Africa. I've never even visited her there.

JOSIE.   But you do see her?

JOE.   When she comes to England, yes.

JOSIE.   How often? How often does she do that?

JOE.   Once or twice a year.

JOSIE.   Where? Where in England do you see her? At your house?

JOE.   No. Rosa, my wife, doesn't — they don't get on. So my mother's never stayed with us.

JOSIE.   So, when you want to see your mother, where do you see her?

JOE.   Airports, restaurants, hotels.

JOSIE.   And at your sister's?

JOE.   My stepsister. My father died, my mother remarried.

JOSIE.   Where does she live?

JOE.   Sussex. But I haven't seen her for some time.

JOSIE.   Christmas two years ago. Where was she living?

JOE.   Sandhurst.

JOSIE.   And you told us you hadn't been in touch with the Army since you bought yourself out in 1968.

JOE.   It was a family matter; my mother was spending Christmas at Sandhurst with Alice.

JOSIE.   And six months after that? You went back to Sandhurst but your mother wasn't there.

JOE.   I had to visit Alice again. It had to do with my mother's will. I'm an executor.

JOSIE.   What rank is your sister's husband?

JOE.   He's a colonel.

JOSIE.   Your wife was with you.

JOE.   Yes, I always took her with me when I went to visit them. I don't really get on with my family and my wife has the facility to talk to anyone.

JOSIE.   Except your mother?

JOE.   My mother's a difficult woman.

JOSIE.   And there was no difficulty with Rosa being Irish?

JOE.   My father was Irish.

JOSIE.   *(Appears to find this funny, but continues.)* Your wife is a Catholic from Derry.

JOE.   Yes.

JOSIE.   Your brother-in-law was in Derry in 'sixty-nine. The then Captain Blakemore was attached to the officer responsible there for releasing 350 CS gas canisters to the police in one night for use against the people of the Bogside — where your wife and her family lived at the time.

JOE.   You can't lay that decision at the door of an Army officer. That's a political decision!

JOSIE.   Not the point of my question. How did your wife get on with the Colonel, given this inconvenient piece of history?

JOE.   Rosa, my wife, never talked to the Colonel. She talked to my sister. They never discussed politics.

JOSIE.   What did she talk to your sister about?

JOE.   Cooking.

JOSIE.   Cooking?

JOE.   Yes. Rosa loved cooking. Alice hated it. So Rosa did the cooking when we stayed there.

JOSIE.   You say you have an arrangement with your wife. I think you mean that she left you.

JOE.   We split up.

JOSIE.   She left you three months after that last visit to Sandhurst.

JOE.   Yes.

JOSIE. Why?

JOE.   I don't know. *(Sighs.)*

JOSIE.   What reason did she give you?

JOE.   None. She couldn't. She didn't say anything. *(Josie gets up from the table and walks to the door of the room, as if to leave.)*

JOSIE.   I don't think you can realize the seriousness of the position you are in. You approached us six months ago offering us your services as a political adviser. We declined because we said we only accept that kind of advice from inside this organization. You then, as we hoped, reapplied to be an active and trained volunteer. Now, at present, as a result of our own investigations, you are under suspicion of attempting to infiltrate us as an agent of British Intelligence. If you don't deal with those suspicions, I am going to walk out of here in a few minutes' time and leave you to your fate.

JOE.   But I don't know how to clear myself. You knew about my Army background. I never attempted to hide that. It was partly an asset to you.

JOSIE.   Your training, yes. We knew you'd left the Army in 'sixty-eight. But what you never told us was that you visited

Sandhurst Military Training Academy on several occasions in the past two years. And previously, Warminster, Bodmin and Osnabruck.

JOE. Exactly where my sister was based each time.

JOSIE. On the last occasion, eighteen months ago, after a visit to Sandhurst your wife left you. At exactly the same time Commander Kitson was also at Sandhurst. I'm sure I don't need to remind you that Kitson is head of Counter Insurgency Operations for the British Army. Now, did your wife leave you because she realized you were working for Counter Insurgency Operations? We think she did. And all you've been able to offer in reply is that your wife spent her visits to Sandhurst happily acting as a kitchen maid for the family of the man who sent CS gas into her family home in Derry.

JOE. It's not true. She was never happy about going there. She hated it. And I did too. But — I gave her no choice. She even used to cry a lot before she went. And then she'd get there and start talking to Alice. It was like a flood. The sun came out. I never knew how she did it. And because she cheered up, I thought she didn't mind in the end. I really believed everything was all right. I have not been recruited by British Intelligence. They never approached me; in fact it's been quite the opposite since I bought myself out of the Army. I met Rosa, as you know, while I was at university in Dublin. My family never approved of my going back to Ireland. My mother saw it as a rejection of her in going there and leaving the Army as I did. She actually complained once to my sister that I married Rosa to spite her, to make her ashamed. A wee hussy from the Bogside, she called her. In marrying Rosa I was also a security risk. My sister even suggested to me that her husband would probably never be made a colonel because of my connections with the wrong side in the Irish War. Not one member of my family came to the wedding. The Army of course refused permission to the Blakemores to attend, something to do with Rosa's part in the Bogside Riots of 'sixty-nine. She was a member of the Citizens' Defence Committee and her name was on the list of conditions which she handed to the Army on their arrival in Derry prior to dismantling the barricades. One of the conditions was a general amnesty for all those people defending their homes in the barricaded area. The barricades came down. However the Army Council and Blakemore's superiors still regarded my wife as a rioter. *(Pause.)* There is one thing you should know. Eighteen months ago at Sandhurst, I did try to meet Kitson. I asked Blakemore to arrange a meeting for me. I had very selfish reasons for doing so. I wanted to interview him for a paper I was giving at a conference in Stockholm on Insecuriy and the State. It would have been a great coup. When I suggested a drink with Kitson either at the mess or at the house, Blakemore refused point blank. My brother-in-law doesn't like him — Kitson has no small talk. My family has nothing but. *(Pause.)* When Rosa left me, she said she regarded all her association with me as a betrayal of her tribe. I really didn't know what she meant at the time. I was deeply mortified and ashamed. Because I do believe she was happy with me once. *(A long pause. Then Josie comes back to the table.)*

JOSIE.   Joe. *(Joe looks up.)* It's finished. *(She picks up the file and puts it back in her bag. She holds out her hand to him.)* Welcome. To the tribe. *(Joe gets to his feet half-dazed. She walks quickly away, followed by Joe. A door bangs. They have gone, the room is in darkness. Someone strikes a match, and we are alerted to the presence of two men. Malachy lights a cigarette for Cathal O'Donnell.)*

MALACHY.   Well, Cathal, I think we have a new man.

O'DONNELL.   I must stop this. *(Holding the lighted cigarette out for inspection.)* Filthy habit. The wife — doesn't approve.

ACT TWO

Scene 1

Donna, Liam, Josie.

Donna is sitting on a straight-backed chair, alone in the living room. There is a light on her face, the rest is darkness.

DONNA.   The devil's back. He was lying with his head on my pillow this morning. When I woke up I recognized him immediately. Even though it's been years. *(Pause.)* The first time I ever saw him, he was standing in the corner of the room. I could feel something watching me. I had the bedclothes tucked up almost to my nose, so that I had to peer carefully round the room — and there he was. He seemed to grow out of the corner until he was towering over me. I panicked because I felt I was suffocating. My first husband was with me at the time. He called a doctor. He said I had asthma. The funny thing was, I really didn't get over my asthma attacks until my husband was interned. And I haven't seen the devil since. *(Pause.)* Until this morning. Liam bent over and kissed me good-bye as he was leaving. The trouble was he blocked my mouth and I couldn't breathe through my nose so I kept having to break away from him. When he'd gone, I closed my eyes and tried to get some sleep before the child woke. That was when I heard the door open. I thought Liam had come back so I opened my eyes, and there he was, the devil. If he had any hair at all it was red. He climbed on top of the bed and put his head on the pillow next to me. I felt so sick at the sight of him because I knew I didn't have the strength to struggle any more. I said: "Please leave me alone." I was very surprised when he replied. He's never spoken to me before. He said very quietly, "All right, Donna." And do you know — he vanished. But I don't believe he's really gone. He never really goes away. *(She begins to have an attack. She starts to vomit or choke twice, but noth-*

47

ing happens. Recovers. The door opens into the room, throwing light across the floor. A figure stands in the light of the doorway.) Who is it?

LIAM.   Who were you expecting? *(He switches on the light and closes the door. Almost tripping over luggage he crosses the room.)* What's this? Are you leaving me?

DONNA.   I told you — Josie's moving back home.

LIAM.   What's the matter with you?

DONNA.   I'm tired.

LIAM.   You're tired all the time now. I think maybe you're tired of me.

DONNA.   Liam, what are you saying?

LIAM.   It's been three weeks since I came out of the Kesh, and all I hear is that you're tired.

DONNA.   Catherine kept me awake all night. I'm exhausted.

LIAM.   You were never exhausted with your husband! *(Donna rushes around the room closing the doors.)*

DONNA.   Please don't fight with me in front of Josie.

LIAM.   *(Raising his voice.)* I'm not fighting with you.

DONNA.   Please don't shout. She'll hear you. I'll feel so humiliated.

LIAM.   But it's true. It's him you want.

DONNA.   Please, Liam. Please lower your voice. She'll think you don't love me and then it'll be difficult for me to feel good about myself and I'll have to leave here for shame and I've nowhere else to go.

LIAM.   Go on, say it. I revolt you. You can't stand the sight of me.

DONNA.   Oh Jesus God, I wish I were dead.

LIAM.   It's true, admit it. Admit it. It's him, isn't it?

DONNA.   No. No. I've loved only you. I always loved only you.

LIAM.   But you married him!

DONNA.   You've got to stop tormenting me because I had a husband. I was a girl then!

LIAM.   Why don't you love me Donna?

DONNA.   I cried all the way up the aisle. I told you that before. I was pregnant, they made me marry him. He was fifteen years older than me. I told him, I didn't love him. He said, "Try

48

to love me, then one day you will." But I couldn't, because I'd always loved you. Oh, I did ever since I was a child. *(Liam is utterly immobile and unmoved during her entreaty.)* Oh Liam, remember I used to come and have my bath with Josie and Frieda on Friday nights. And you used to pretend not to notice us. And then one Friday night you came into the parlour and said, "What's happening?" And we said we were having a party and we were putting our money together for lemonade and crisps and you said, "Well, here's some silver towards your party." And Josie said you'd never given them a penny before towards anything. It was because I was there. And I blushed and laughed. Oh, I've loved you since I was nine years old. *(For the first time he turns to her.)*

LIAM.   But you married him!

DONNA.   Oh Liam. Liam! You know why.

LIAM.   You had him first.

DONNA.   You went away! You went away that summer!

LIAM.   I had work to do.

DONNA.   But you went away, you went to the Republic.

LIAM.   I was wanted. We feared internment.

DONNA.   And when you came back you had a girlfriend from Dublin. God, you had so many. I started going with Peter McNamee after that because I was lonely and he was kind to me. I left him for you. I gave up my son for you. As soon as you wanted me, I came. What more can I do?

LIAM.   It wasn't just McNamee. There were others. They told me. They'd all had you. After the dances.

DONNA.   Oh Jesus God!

LIAM.   In the Kesh they told me about you after the dances. They all had you. But now you don't want me! Were they better than me, was that it? *(Donna takes up a knife from the table, and hands it to him.)*

DONNA.   Take it. Kill me, love. Kill me. Kill me.

LIAM.   No!

DONNA.   Kill me. You want to kill me. Please.

LIAM.   No! *(He throws the knife away.)*

DONNA.   I can't do any more. I love you. I have always loved you. I gave away my only son for you. Because he looked like

Peter. If you don't believe that I love you — I wish I were dead.
I wish I were dead.

LIAM.   Don't say that, Donna.

DONNA.   I wish I were dead.

LIAM.   I just had to find out. *(Liam ruffles her hair.)* I love you
so much you see. And I can't get enough of you. When I'm
away, things prey on my mind. I kept remembering all those
years before we went out together and all the other men in
your life. And I thought because I'm not around so much
you'd find someone else.

DONNA.   I won't find anyone else. I promise. You mean everything to me.

LIAM.   I'd like to go to bed now.

DONNA.   I can't! Josie's upstairs.

LIAM.   *(Becoming cold again.)* All right. I'll be back in an hour.

DONNA.   Liam! Please. Where are you going?

LIAM.   I'm going to the Club! *(He leaves, slamming the door.
Donna sinks down, beginning to cry; only Josie's rapid footsteps on the
stair force her to pull herself together.)*

JOSIE.   *(Bursts open the door from the stairway carrying an armful
of dresses on hangers.)* Was that our Liam? *(Donna nods. Josie leaves
the dresses over the cases.)* I was hoping for a lift. He uses this
place like a cloakroom. *(Coming back to Donna.)* My daddy'll be
along later to pick this stuff up.

DONNA.   I wish you weren't going.

JOSIE.   So do I. I'm dreading it. He treats me like a kid!

DONNA.   Why don't you stay?

JOSIE.   Three's a crowd. Anyway, I think you and Liam need
time together. You should have a wee holiday.

DONNA.   Yes, I know. He said he would take us away somewhere hot. Where are you off to now?

JOSIE.   Dublin for the weekend — with Joe Conran.

DONNA.   Do you see much of him?

JOSIE.   We're working together. *(Hurrying.)* Bye-bye. *(She kisses
Donna.)*

DONNA.   Nice perfume. Lemons?

JOSIE.   Joe gave it to me. He got it duty free on his last trip to Amsterdam.

DONNA.   What are you getting so defensive about? I just said you smelt of lemons.

JOSIE.   *(At the door.)* What'll I bring you back from Dublin?

DONNA.   *(Waving her away.)* Yourself.

JOSIE.   I'll see you. *(Josie smiles and leaves the room. Donna is smiling as well.)*

Scene 2

McDermot, Frieda.

A room in John McDermot's house. He is on the telephone. The clasped hands symbol of the Party is on the wall, along with the slogan: "Democracy against Direct Rule." The room reflects that his political commitment is not separate from his domestic arrangements. The telephone cradle stands on a chair.

McDERMOT.   Well, obviously it's very dangerous, it will set back the cause of Irish unity another — *(Pause.)* You're not interested in Irish unity? Thank you. *(Frieda arrives with a handful of leaflets. She has been outside. McDermot puts down the phone.)* That's the third trade unionist out of seven who refuses to discuss the Petition against the Amendment. It's unbelievable. They've all said the same thing — no interest in the politics of the Republic.

FRIEDA.   What's the Petition against the Amendment?

McDERMOT.   *(Going towards her.)* Do you mean to tell me that you haven't even read the leaflets you're handing out?

FRIEDA.   I was rushing.

McDERMOT.   That's no excuse.

FRIEDA.   Och, what is it about? It'll save me reading it. I hate political pamphlets. Anyway, you always explain things better than you write them.

McDERMOT.   I don't think there's anybody who has insulted

51

me more than you have — in my life.

FRIEDA. You're awful easy insulted. I'm the same with everybody.

McDERMOT. *(Sighs.)* There's to be a referendum in the Republic to decide whether the Constitution should be amended to include an anti-abortion clause. Abortion is already illegal in the South; by putting it into the Constitution it cannot be challenged or even changed. Do you see? It's the Catholic Church barricading itself into the Constitution.

FRIEDA. *(Putting the leaflet down.)* I wouldn't sign that petition.

McDERMOT. You don't agree with abortion as a civil right for Protestants in the South?

FRIEDA. I don't really regard the politics of Southern Ireland as having anything to do with me.

McDERMOT. Well, that is truly extraordinary.

FRIEDA. It's a foreign country as far as I'm concerned.

McDERMOT. I think you're taking your rebellion against your father a bit far. Surely you want a united Ireland by democratic consent?

FRIEDA. No, it's not even that, I just don't care if Ireland is united or not.

McDERMOT. What do you care about?

FRIEDA. I just want to sing my own songs.

McDERMOT. *(Ironic.)* Is that all?

FRIEDA. *(Misunderstanding.)* It's everything. When the lights go down and I'm standing in a spotlight. There's a tremor; it starts in my toes and roots me to the floor when the first note comes. I'm pulled away to somewhere else entirely. There's nothing like it. Except that I want to do it again and again.

McDERMOT. I used to feel like that a long time ago when I made — political speeches. But I don't any more. Maybe it's the size of the audience these days. *(Pause.)* Have you ever cared about a person the way you care about singing?

FRIEDA. I don't believe in love, if that's what you mean.

McDERMOT. What about caring for a friend? A person? *(Frieda shakes her head.)* You see, I'm in politics because I care for people. But I care most of all for one person, and have for some time. Frieda, I care about you.

FRIEDA.   Don't say that! I'll only disappoint you. *(He takes advantage of her confusion and kisses her. She responds momentarily, and then breaks away.)* Oh I hate you!

McDERMOT.   No, you don't.

FRIEDA.   I do. You've gone and spoiled everything.

McDERMOT.   You wanted me to spoil it. You were furious when my girlfriend came out of the bathroom the other morning.

FRIEDA.   That was because she was having a bath when I wanted a pee.

McDERMOT.   And you were very annoyed when I stayed away last night. All night.

FRIEDA.   Ha! The vanity of it!

McDERMOT.   You sulked all through breakfast. In fact you manage to sulk every time I bring a woman into the house. I can't persuade anyone to spend the night any more because your hostility makes them so uncomfortable.

FRIEDA.   If that's what you think, there is a solution.

McDERMOT.   I think so, too.

FRIEDA.   I'd better move out.

McDERMOT.   Alternatively I could kiss you again, and we could go to bed this afternoon.

FRIEDA.   You're smiling.

McDERMOT.   I've been smiling from the beginning. And I've wanted you for a long time. Why do you think I invited you to stay with me? *(He attempts to kiss her again, but she moves away immediately.)*

FRIEDA.   I can't. You're my friend. You're the only friend I've got now. If I sleep with you, you won't be my friend any more. And I'll have to find somewhere else to live. And frankly, I don't feel like it.

McDERMOT.   What are you afraid of?

FRIEDA.   I'm not afraid. *(Furious.)* I've never run away from anything in my life.

McDERMOT.   You've never run away from a fight. But there are other areas of experience. *(Makes another attempt to touch her.)* Frieda, *(Very kindly.)* I'm very good in bed.

53

FRIEDA. *(Enraged. Hits him in the chest.)* I hate you, John Mc-Dermot. *(She throws the pamphlets across the room and exits.)*
McDERMOT. Frieda! What did I say? *(The phone rings. McDermot is not sure whether to pick it up.)* Frieda! Please come back! *(The phone rings until he picks it up.)* Hello? ... Yes, this is John McDermot ... yes, I did call you earlier ... It's about the Petition against the Amendment. I'm collecting signatures from prominent trade unionists and people like yourself. It's for an open letter we want to publish in the *Irish Times* ... *(Frieda arrives with a suitcase. He begins to signal to her while talking on the phone, but she refuses to respond.)* What's that? ... Look, can I ring you back? ... You've caught me at a difficult moment ... Yes, of course ... Good-bye. *(Puts the phone down.)*
FRIEDA. Can I use that phone please? I want to ring for a taxi.
McDERMOT. What are you doing? *(She sits down on her suitcase.)* I thought you didn't want to be homeless.
FRIEDA. I find your confidence both in relation to me, other women, and the rest of the world nothing short of nauseous. You behave as if you had nothing to learn, nothing to discover, no problems, and everybody else was waiting for you to fuck them!
McDERMOT. I'm sure you're right.
FRIEDA. But what I really hate is the idea of having to trade something for my being here.
McDERMOT. My intention wasn't to trade. I wanted you. And I didn't repress it. That's all. The house is yours; there's no price. *(She proceeds to pick up the phone book. He seems about to leave the room and give up, when he stops.)* Where will you go?
FRIEDA. As far away from you as possible. I'll resign from the Party.
McDERMOT. And what reason will you give for that?
FRIEDA. Personal reasons.
McDERMOT. There are no personal reasons any more. Everything is political.
FRIEDA. I've heard that before!
McDERMOT. When you joined the Party you promised to secure working class unity — Catholic and Protestant — before

the real struggle could begin. I can't see that my personal be-
haviour towards you should make any difference to your commitment to that idea.

FRIEDA. On the contrary, I tend to judge ideas by the people who utter them.

McDERMOT. *(Sighs.)* That's just the trouble, Frieda. Your
standards arc so high. *(She is arrested by the remark for a moment.
Then she closes the telephone book, puts it down and reaches for the
phone. Beginning to dial the number.)* Frieda. *(He stops her.)* Listen
to me. I'll miss you. I'll miss you messing up the house. I'll miss
you leaving all the dishes for me to wash. Leaving all the lights
on. Running up the heating bills. I'll miss you letting the fire
go out, and then not being able to relight it. I'll miss your awful
singing in the bath. Being rude to my friends, particularly
when they're women. Most of all I'll miss the way you change
your mind. You're so much trouble, Frieda, would you do one
thing — one thing I wouldn't miss?

FRIEDA. What?

McDERMOT. Would you stay?

FRIEDA. *(Overcome. Moving towards him.)* Do I really annoy you
that much?

McDERMOT. Yes.

FRIEDA. Am I really that much trouble?

McDERMOT. Yes. *(They kiss, for a long time.)*

Scene 3

Josie, Joe.

*Dublin. A hotel bedroom. Josie is sitting up on the bed staring
at an eighteenth-century doorway. Joe is lying back, listening
sleepily.*

JOSIE. It's strange you bringing me here.

JOE. Why?

JOSIE. That time I told you about, when I first came to Dublin, I walked round for hours just looking at the place. I passed

this hotel but I didn't notice it. I had my head down against the rain until a glass coach drew up alongside me.

JOE. And a beautiful girl got out wearing glass slippers!

JOSIE. There was a bride and groom in it. They were coming in here. There were some people in gold braid on the steps, they were standing on red carpet, through the window you could see the chandeliers, and above it all a tricolour was flying … It was the same flag that one July my father flew from our upstairs window. I'd have braved a baton charge to get that flag back from the police who snatched it. And I did … Yet nothing in the world would have induced me to defy the grandness of this place. I felt as if they'd snatched the flag away again … That's why it's so strange you bringing me here.

JOE. I can't imagine you lacking in courage, Josie.

JOSIE. Oh, I frequently do … Have you ever killed anyone? *(He begins to sit up.)*

JOE. I can't say that I have.

JOSIE. Not even as a soldier?

JOE. I trained as an engineer.

JOSIE. Oh yes.

JOE. Have you ever killed anyone?

JOSIE. I planted a bomb once. It didn't go off.

JOE. Why?

JOSIE. I don't know, some technical fault.

JOE. No, I mean why did you plant a bomb?

JOSIE. I was fed up being a courier … They used women as messengers then. I wanted to show them I could take the same risks as a man. So I planned it, stole the car, and left it outside the law courts. I'm glad it didn't go off.

JOE. You did this entirely on your own?

JOSIE. No. A man I'd have gone to hell for helped me.

JOE. When was this?

JOSIE. In the early seventies. We were all a little bit mad then. Me especially.

JOE. So you wouldn't do it again?

JOSIE. I've lost the killing instinct. Now, I tend to think the crushing of a foetus is a tragedy.

JOE. Well, that's up to you.

JOSIE. Have you ever loved anyone so much you would die for them?

JOE. This is fun, Josie. I want what there is between us to begin and end in this room. And then on another occasion we could go to another room and have some more fun.

JOSIE. Fun! I hate that word. *(He reaches out to stroke her hair.)*

JOE. I'm sorry if I offended you. *(He kisses her.)* Do you know him well?

JOSIE. Who?

JOE. O'Donnell.

JOSIE. He taught me how to build a barricade. *(She looks at her watch.)* And he doesn't like to be kept waiting. *(Joe gets out of bed, goes to the bathroom en suite, leaving the door open. Immediate sound of ablutions. Josie herself entirely alone. The sound of ablutions gradually fades as she begins to speak. Speaking aloud.)* Bus stop posts; manhole covers; telephone kiosk doors; traffic signs; corrugated iron fencing; and old doors, wood is best not glass; especially if you don't have an upturned bus or lorry. And a tape measure is useful too, to measure the mouth of the street … He held one end of the tape and I had the other. It was the first time I'd ever seen him. He kept shouting at me to hold still. Hurry up. Move quickly. Find the rope, nails, wood. He was so precise. And I kept coming back with what he wanted every time … All day we ran about measuring, hammering, securing, until towards evening we needed only two slim posts and it was finished. I remember we rushed off to the park to uproot some young trees, saplings the Corporation planted. We were high up on the bank when a woman passed. She was pushing a pram; a pregnant woman in a headscarf, then she waved. It was my first whole day with him. "It's my wife," he said. Safe. I'm safe from him. The sight of her large and alone, thoughts on her child in the womb and in the pram were battleship enough to keep me away. Until minutes later I slipped, slid down the wet bank after him and came to a halt. "I can't get down," I said. And he reached out his hand … I wasn't safe. I was lost. *(Joe returns, dressed. He watches from the doorway.)*

Scene 4

Frieda, McDermot, First Policeman, Second Policeman.

*Two swings. A litter bin. Sounds of a children's playground.
Frieda comes on.*

FRIEDA.   This is a good place. *(Looking skyward. McDermot comes
on, also looking skyward.)* There'll be hundreds here. *(Running
with her hands outstretched.)* This one's mine. *(Pause.)* How many
have you got?
McDERMOT.   I wasn't counting.
FRIEDA.   You've got to count them. That's the whole point.
McDERMOT.   I'm not very good at this. It's not easy.
FRIEDA.   Listen …
McDERMOT.   It's too calm. *(She looks round. He takes a notebook
out of his pocket to write in.)*
FRIEDA.   Ah you're not going to do that again. *(He walks away
to the swing and sits down.)*
McDERMOT.   There's not enough wind.
FRIEDA.   It won't be long. *(She follows him and sits down on the
second swing.)* What is it anyway?
McDERMOT.   A piece for the paper on the by-election in Area
H.
FRIEDA.   Where's Area H?
McDERMOT.   North Belfast.
FRIEDA.   Why can't they call it that? Why do you have to be
a computer these days before you get any information? *(Pause.
Waiting.)* How did we do?
McDERMOT.   Four hundred and seventy-four votes out of a
total poll of 6,881. Seven percent of the poll. Not bad. We seem
to be a growing force in the north of the city.
FRIEDA.   John … there was a man following me in the rose
gardens. I wasn't taking much notice — and then everywhere
I turned he seemed to follow. When I stopped, he stopped. He

58

was blocking the only way out. I had to run through the rose beds to get away from him.

McDERMOT.   Where was I when this was happening?

FRIEDA.   I think you were in the Tropical Ravine. My arms are all scratched!

McDERMOT.   I suppose you thought he wanted to assault you? Not everybody does you know.

FRIEDA.   He wasn't looking at me like that. He frightened me! His eyes were like ice. It felt as if he were deliberately marking me.

McDERMOT.   Why would he do that?

FRIEDA.   Intimidation!

McDERMOT.   Your head's cut! This is a university district. It's always been safe.

FRIEDA.   For some people nowhere is safe. *(Suddenly looks up.)* Oh look! We're missing our chance. *(She gets up from the swing and runs forward, looking skyward, her arms outstretched, hands cupped.)* I've got one. *(She runs first to the L. a little, then to the R., as if chasing something. Claps her hands suddenly.)* Missed! *(McDermot starts up.)*

McDERMOT.   I see one. *(He runs forward, towards it, and then follows it off. Voice off. Claps hands.)* Got it!

FRIEDA.   Oh, I see another. *(She follows it as before, running about. She claps her hands together.)* Missed it! Damn! *(A Landrover screeches to a halt. Door slams. A Policeman in a bullet-proof jacket approaches Frieda, who is standing with her eyes trained skyward.)*

FIRST POLICEMAN.   What's going on here? *(Frieda starts to rush off.)*

FRIEDA.   There's another gust of wind — *(The Policeman grabs her arm.)*

FIRST POLICEMAN.   I'm speaking to you.

FRIEDA.   *(Indignant.)* Shit! I've lost it. *(McDermot appears, holding his head.)*

McDERMOT.   I nearly knocked myself out that time. *(A Second Policeman in a bullet-proof jacket approaches. He too is looking skyward. Everyone is looking skyward.)*

SECOND POLICEMAN.   Is there something up there? *(Every-*

59

one looks at Frieda.)
FRIEDA. Yes. Leaves.
FIRST POLICEMAN. Leaves?
FRIEDA. Yeah. It's autumn and the leaves are falling. So what you have to do is stand under a really big tree and wait till they fall.
SECOND POLICEMAN. Why?
FRIEDA. You have to try and catch them before they reach the ground. And for every one you catch you have one happy day next year. So I was standing here trying to catch three hundred and sixty-five, before you came along. *(She looks skyward again.)*
FIRST POLICEMAN. Are you trying to make a fool of us?
McDERMOT. No. Look. We're terribly sorry. She was a bit depressed, so we thought we'd come out and catch a few leaves to cheer her up!
FIRST POLICEMAN. You realize you're causing an obstruction.
FRIEDA. *(Looking up.)* That's the intention.
FIRST POLICEMAN. We've had a number of complaints from the residents here that you two people have been causing a disturbance.
SECOND POLICEMAN. Do you live around here?
McDERMOT. We live close by. We didn't realize we'd upset anyone. We'll go home now. Come on, Frieda. *(He begins to take her away. She stops.)*
FRIEDA. Wait a minute. Do they not know about catching leaves, the people who complained about us?
SECOND POLICEMAN. Go on home now. Before you cause any more trouble.
McDERMOT. Come on, Frieda.
FRIEDA. Trouble? Is it trouble to want to be happy? Do you not know about catching leaves? Do you not remember? *(McDermot and Frieda go. The First Policeman goes off in the opposite direction. The Second Policeman looks up skyward for a moment. Sound of a Landrover engine starting. He too hurries off. A leaf flutters down.)*

Scene 5

Donna, Josie, First Soldier, Second Soldier, Policeman.

Donna's living room. There is a glass of red wine on a low table and a bottle of pills. A small child's toy, a musical ball, is on the floor.

Donna comes into the room followed by Josie.

JOSIE. Liam said you were upset.

DONNA. Upset? Catherine fell down the stairs. Her head must have hit every step on the way down. Liam was right behind her. He couldn't stop it.

JOSIE. Is she all right?

DONNA. I sometimes think men don't actually like children — she's all right. She's made of rubber. I feel sick every time I think of it.

JOSIE. What are the pills for?

DONNA. The doctor gave me them — to calm me down.

JOSIE. Donna, I've something to tell you.

DONNA. Has he left his wife for you yet?

JOSIE. She left him ages ago.

DONNA. She's a braver woman than I thought. She's eight months pregnant.

JOSIE. Where did you hear that?

DONNA. Everybody knows Mairead O'Donnell's pregnant.

JOSIE. Not Cathal! I was talking about Joe.

DONNA. I can't keep up with this! Three months ago you had my head turned — you were so passionately in love with Cathal O'Donnell.

JOSIE. I know, but … have you ever thought, is this the man who has come to love me?

DONNA. You're not wise.

JOSIE. Oh Donna. I owe him so much. I'm really beginning to feel healed. I even forgot about Cathal. He took all the pain

61

away! *(Catherine begins to cry. Donna goes to the door and listens. It stops. Then crying continues.)*

DONNA. I'm in for a bad night. *(She exits. Josie listens also. Voice off.)* All right, lamb pie. Mammy's coming! *(Josie, very thoughtful, picks up the musical ball. It tinkles gently when lifted, and again as she moves it at her ear.)*

JOSIE. Fuck! *(Drops it.)* Donna! It's the Brits. *(Donna runs back into the room.)*

DONNA. Get out! Leave me!

JOSIE. Can you cope?

DONNA. Leave me! They can't take me away if there's nobody to look after the child. *(Josie exits quickly through the front door, which she doesn't have time to close. The sound of Landrovers screeching to a halt and doors slamming, followed by heavily shod feet running. Donna takes up the bottle of pills in time to face the first of two armed soldiers who come through the open door.)* Where are the RUC? You're not allowed to raid our houses without a member of the police being present.

FIRST SOLDIER. Don't get smart. *(A Policeman enters, and waits quietly in the background. The Second Soldier begins to look around.)* Where is he? *(Donna watches the Soldier who has gone out to search the rooms.)*

DONNA. Don't waken the child. Where's who?

FIRST SOLDIER. Your husband.

DONNA. My husband's in the Crumlin Road Gaol. I haven't seen him for ten years.

POLICEMAN. We're looking for Liam McCoy.

DONNA. I don't know. I haven't seen him.

POLICEMAN. He lives here.

DONNA. Only when it suits him.

FIRST SOLDIER. So where is he?

DONNA. I don't know. You know what it's like. He goes out, gets drunk and forgets to come back. It's not against the law you know. *(The Second Soldier comes back. He's carrying two small firearms in a towel. He presents it to her.)* You planted it.

SECOND SOLDIER. *(To the First Soldier.)* Loose floorboard at the top of the stairs.

FIRST SOLDIER.   You could do three years for this.

DONNA.   How could I do three years? You won't find my prints on them.

FIRST SOLDIER.   *(To the Policeman.)* What about that other address? *(The Policeman hands him a piece of paper.)* Two-six-two Grosvenor Road. *(They wait for Donna's reaction.)* Maybe she knows where he is.

SECOND SOLDIER.   Must be with Eileen tonight.

FIRST SOLDIER.   Have you met Eileen? Dark hair. Slim. Very nice. Sure you don't know her? *(Bin lids start up.)*

DONNA.   Get out! Get out of my house! *(Catherine begins to cry loudly.)*

SECOND SOLDIER.   I'm sure Eileen knows where he is?

DONNA.   If you don't leave me alone I'll take these pills. I mean it. I'll swallow the lot! *(She puts the bottle to her mouth and begins to swallow the pills. Some fall on the floor, scattering.)*

POLICEMAN.   *(Coming forward.)* Hey, hey. *(The Soldiers withdraw quickly.)* Now, now. Nobody's going to harm you. It's your man they're after. *(The bin lids die down with the Soldiers' exit. Donna stops, looks round at the Policeman. Catherine cries out again.)* What age is the baby?

DONNA.   Fuck off! *(The Policeman exits. Donna sits down and pours the rest of the pills into her hand; she looks at the glass of wine. Catherine's crying reaches a pitch of screaming. The bin lids get louder. Darkness. Every sound stops.)*

Scene 6

Josie, O'Donnell, Liam, Malachy, Danny, Donna.

The Club. A room off the main bar. Cathal O'Donnell is sitting at a small café table. The scene is similar to the room arrangement when Josie interrogated Joe Conran. There is an empty chair opposite Cathal; he seems to be waiting. Josie comes in. She has not expected to find herself alone with O'Donnell.

JOSIE.   I was told my brother was here.

O'DONNELL.   He's all right.

JOSIE.   Donna's house was raided.

O'DONNELL.   Yes, we heard.

JOSIE.   I think someone should go and see if she's all right. I wasn't able to go back. *(Pause.)* I suppose he realizes that he can't go home. *(She turns to go.)*

O'DONNELL.   Josie!

JOSIE.   I've got to find Joe — I don't want him walking into a patrol.

O'DONNELL.   He's gone home. I want to talk to you.

JOSIE.   So I hear.

O'DONNELL.   Did Joe tell you about his assignment?

JOSIE.   No. Of course not!

O'DONNELL.   That's very professional of him.

JOSIE.   He is — I cleared him, remember.

O'DONNELL.   Oh yes ... So you think it's an impossibility? *(She looks confused.)* The thirty-two-county workers' republic. A place we will never come into.

JOSIE.   You were there!

O'DONNELL.   You never said that to me.

JOSIE.   You don't trust anyone. Do you Cathal?

O'DONNELL.   You do yourself an injustice. I wanted to see him. I thought if I could see him — I would know.

JOSIE.   And do you?

O'DONNELL.   Yes. It's really very simple. He's a romantic. Sit down. *(Pause. Josie sits reluctantly. O'Donnell immediately gets to his feet.)* I've put Conran in charge of arms purchasing. The whole operation. And stockpiling for the period after British Withdrawal. That's why I wanted to talk to you. He's going to meet the Libyans in Malta next month. The idea is that he will do the buying abroad but I'd like you to find the locations in Ireland where the stuff can be kept until it's needed. *(Pause.)* Well, are you happy about that? Do you see any problems?

JOSIE.   Since when has my happiness been a priority of yours?

O'DONNELL.   Oh I see. You're going to be vengeful.

JOSIE.   I'm not going to be vengeful. My wounds are healed. But I am just a little surprised and suspicious that I am being

64

consulted about something I am usually told to do. *(O'Donnell sits down again opposite her.)*

O'DONNELL.   Are we talking about this assignment or are we talking about something else? If we're talking about your assignments, you have always been consulted by me. I have always taken your advice. I have always trusted your instincts and your judgement. If we're talking about something else, then I suggest that you say so. But don't infect your political judgement with emotional considerations!

JOSIE.   You were never very keen to separate them before.

O'DONNELL.   I did try to talk to you in Dublin, but you ran away from me.

JOSIE.   You know damn well what I'm complaining about. Your interest in me was to do with your desires, your appetites, your needs, which were fortunately once coincidental with mine. Now they're clearly not!

O'DONNELL.   Once? Once coincidental?

JOSIE.   Yes. They ceased to coincide when you let go of me five months ago!

O'DONNELL.   Not for me.

JOSIE.   Oh please. You cut me off! You sat at meetings ignoring me. You made sure that you and I were never alone. I got my orders through other people all of a sudden. You put the whole power of this organization between us, so I could never get a chance to ask you why. For ten years you have been my only lover, and because it was never publicly acknowledged no one ever understood my grief. *(Pause.)* You came out of that meeting in Dublin and you said, "Are you around?" What did you expect me to say? "Yes." For your pleasure?

O'DONNELL.   Five months ago I had to leave you and return to my wife. She was pregnant again. As you know, her last pregnancy miscarried. She has no family, unlike you. She has no one to turn to but me. She depends on me totally. And she's tenaciously loyal. Because I was sent word that she'd been so ill, and because of being married to me, she was having a very difficult time — the house was raided twice in a month — I came north to take her back across the border. It was not easy for me to stop seeing you, but there was nothing else for it.

Since Mairead and I have been living together again I redis-covered what I'd forgotten — that my wife is not the passion in my life, you are. I once told you that I'd never let you down.

JOSIE.   You said you'd never let her down either.

O'DONNELL.   I intend to keep my promise. I don't intend to choose between you.

JOSIE.   I'm afraid you'll have to.

O'DONNELL.   I can't live without you. I have tried. I fought the memory of you every day. But you are the one who is with me in my thoughts all the time, not her; it's your voice I want to hear when she speaks, not hers.

JOSIE.   I've begun again with someone else.

O'DONNELL.   I can't let you go. It's not over.

JOSIE.   (Almost laughing.) Oh, it's not over. For months there was no one. Until Joe Conran appears. Then suddenly you no-tice, and it's not over! Well, it is for me.

O'DONNELL.   I understand why you're with him. But you also need me. I see no reason why our friendship shouldn't con-tinue. I don't let go of my friends easily. (Josie gets up from the table.)

JOSIE.   I hope that's not a threat!

O'DONNELL.   It's not a threat. How could I threaten you when the whole apparatus of the British State doesn't cause you a hair's turn! Josie, I still love you.

JOSIE.   Love? You once told me that to love something was to confer a greater existence on it — you were talking about pa-triotism — the love of your country. I've only recently realized that you never loved me. You took me. You possessed me. You took my youth and you hid it in a dark corner for a long time. You never draped me with a public celebration. But I'm out of the corner. It's over. The hiding is finished. You are in my thoughts from time to time, I admit; but usually as a prelude to a nightmare. (Getting up.) If you've nothing else to say, I'd like to go. I've no wish to discuss "other business" with you. You can send your messages through the usual channels.

O'DONNELL.   All right, Josie. But it's not over yet!

JOSIE.   (Turning.) Six months ago I'd have died for you. Five weeks ago, even, I might have listened. Now — it's too late.

O'DONNELL. Why is it too late? What has so many weeks got to do with it?

JOSIE. I'm going to have his child. *(He is visibly devastated. Relentless.)* I'm pregnant too. *(He attempts a recovery.)*

O'DONNELL. Congratulations.

JOSIE. Thanks. *(She walks away to the exit door. Turns again.)* Good-bye Cathal. *(She exits. He is left alone sitting at the table. He smiles through his teeth, takes a packet of cigarettes from his pocket, stops smiling, crushes the cigarette packet, goes off, passing Malachy and Liam on his way out.)*

LIAM. Was that Cathal?

MALACHY. Aye.

LIAM. What's he looking so pleased about?

MALACHY. He's not. He's got an ulcer; he always smiles when it hurts. *(He puts his empty glass down.)* Will you take another wee drink? *(Liam shakes his head.)* What's wrong with you tonight?

LIAM. I'm worried about Josie. I don't know how you could let her do it.

MALACHY. What else could I do? She said: "I want to go and live with him." I said: "Over my dead body." She said: "I'm having his baby." I said: "Fair enough. I'll help you move." What was I supposed to do? I'm no good with wee babies. *(The two men move down the table with their pint glasses and set them down.)*

LIAM. She hardly knows him.

MALACHY. Well, she'd get to know him better now!

LIAM. You should never have let her move out of the house in the first place.

MALACHY. Don't you lay that at my door. It was your idea that she moved in with Donna. If you hadn't been so paranoid about your wife running off with somebody while you were in the Kesh, Josie would still be at home with me now. *(Donna comes in like a ghost, unseen, and waits.)* At least he's on our side. Not like that other wee bitch running off with a Stickie!

LIAM. We hope he's on our side.

MALACHY. Ah now, don't you start that again. He's off to Malta with four and a half million of our money; you can be sure we checked him out.

LIAM. I just don't trust Conran. It's funny my house being

67

raided.

DONNA.   Your house? *(Both men turn.)*

LIAM.   Donna!

MALACHY.   Would you take a wee drink? *(Senses danger.)* Gabriel's got three tons of sugar. *(Malachy senses danger and exits quickly.)*

LIAM.   *(Pause.)* I'm sorry about what happened. *(She walks up to him and hits him with her fist on the side of the head. The blow stuns him. He reels momentarily. He never takes his eyes off her.)* All right Donna. *(Backing off.)* All right. *(He backs away and then turns and hurries off to another part of the Club. She turns and walks away towards the door out. She stops, puts her hand to her chest, breathing deeply. She appears to vomit or choke once, then twice. Nothing happens. Danny appears quickly at her side. She is bent double and does not see who it is.)*

DANNY.   Donna? Donna? *(She straightens hopefully and discovers him.)* Are you all right?

DONNA.   Yes, I'm fine.

DANNY.   What's wrong?

DONNA.   Nothing. Please go away.

DANNY.   You don't look very happy.

DONNA.   Life's not a bed of roses.

DANNY.   Can I walk you home? Please?

DONNA.   If you like. *(They exit.)*

Scene 7

Josie, Joe.

Bedroom. Joe is packing clothes into a bag. Josie comes into the room in her nightdress.

JOE.   What is it?

JOSIE.   I'm bleeding again.

JOE.   What can I do?

JOSIE.   *(She gets into bed.)* I have to lie down and put my feet up. Can you put a pillow under my feet? *(He puts a pillow under her feet.)* I have to raise them higher than my head. *(She lies back.)* It happened a few days ago; but it stopped when I lay down. It's such a dangerous time … Oh God! I'd be so angry if I lost it.

JOE.   You won't lose it, Josie. I know what that's like. My wife miscarried. *(He lies down beside her.)*

JOSIE.   If you'd had a child with your wife, would you have stayed with her?

JOE.   If, if, if. Who can answer if?

JOSIE.   What's wrong?

JOE.   *(Pause.)* I was thinking about your brother.

JOSIE.   Our Liam?

JOE.   He's not happy.

JOSIE.   Liam's never happy. He's stupid. He's on the run permanently. *(Joe sits up.)*

JOE.   I think he's resentful because I got the assignment he wanted.

JOSIE.   That's right: foreign travel. He promised Donna a continental holiday when he got out of the Kesh.

JOE.   I wish O'Donnell hadn't been so brutal with him. He said I spoke five modern languages, which is an absolute must for working abroad, while Liam only had Gaelic. The last thing I want is to make enemies here —

JOSIE.   Joe! I want out!

JOE.   Out? Out of what?

JOSIE.   I'm tired. Tired of this endless night watch. I've been manning the barricades since 'sixty-nine. I'd like to stop for a while, look around me, plant a garden, listen for other sounds; the breathing of a child somewhere outside Andersonstown.

JOE.   You constantly surprise me.

JOSIE.   Do you know what I spent the last few days worrying about? An incident — the night Donna's house was raided. I was walking back from the Club, there was a foot patrol in the street. I should have turned back immediately and warned the men. But I was so preoccupied I wasn't even aware of the Army until I walked right into them and nearly fell over a corporal sitting in a hawthorn hedge with his face blackened. He shouted something stupid after me like: "This is a great place

69

to come for a holiday." And do you know what I was thinking about? Whether my womb would be big enough for the child. Because you're so big and I'm so small. I'm really worried that the baby might get too big too quickly and come out before it's finished.

JOE. You idiot!

JOSIE. I'm so afraid of losing it. It's like a beginning within me. For the first time the possibility of being happy. So I'm going to tell O'Donnell that I won't accept this or any other assignment.

JOE. Perhaps it's something you feel at the moment.

JOSIE. No. I don't want my mother's life!

JOE. Then why? Why are you having a child? You did this without asking me!

JOSIE. It was my decision — it had nothing to do with you.

JOE. It was our decision!

JOSIE. We grew up by the hearth and slept in cots at the fire. We escaped nothing and nothing escaped us ... I wish I could go back.

JOE. Go back?

JOSIE. Yes, and remember ... those first moments.

JOE. Remember what?

JOSIE. Back then ... somehow rid myself of that dark figure which hovered about the edge of my cot — priest or police I can't tell — but the light is so dim in my memory — most of the room is in shadow — and gets dimmer all the time.

JOE. Josie!

JOSIE. I'm trying to tell you why — about the first few moments when I took the wrong way.

JOE. Josie! It's not what we saw through the bars of a cot or heard from the corner of a nursery that made us what we are.

JOSIE. You would say that.

JOE. It won't help you to remember, because it wasn't so individual.

JOSIE. The bleeding's stopped.

JOE. I came to this country because I tried to live the life you seem to want now. I tried it with someone else and it didn't work.

JOSIE. Rosa. That woman's name haunts me. Did she want children very much? And you didn't? *(He gets off the bed quickly and paces the room.)*
JOE. I hate tots! Babies! I hate this whole fertility business! I'm not interested in fucking children!
JOSIE. *(Pause.)* I don't ask you for anything but to be with me until the birth.
JOE. Of course I'll be with you. But you mustn't depend on me, Rosa — *(Josie stares. Joe realizes.)* Josie. *(He gets into bed beside her.)* Let me hold you ... Look, when I come back from Malta, I'll take you away for a while. *(A long pause.)*
JOSIE. You don't have to worry about me, Joe. I've got two hearts.

Scene 8

Frieda, McDermot.

Bedroom in McDermot's flat in South Belfast.

A cacophony of cymbals, skin drums, tambourines from the street.

FRIEDA. What on earth's that? *(She sits up in bed.)*
McDERMOT. The Chinese restaurant are celebrating their Sabbath.
FRIEDA. It's not very harmonious.
McDERMOT. I think the year of thc rat is about to begin. *(She listens again.)*
FRIEDA. Stop it!
McDERMOT. What?
FRIEDA. Don't be so innocent. You know what you are doing.
McDERMOT. I was just exploring.
FRIEDA. John! ... I've come seven times already, I can't come any more.
McDERMOT. But I thought you liked it.
FRIEDA. I'm all confused. I have so many things to think

71

about … what I'm going to do with my life … where I'm going to go next … I have plans to make but every time you make love to me my mind goes blank!

McDERMOT.   You're tired of me.

FRIEDA.   Maybe I'm not just what you want, John … I want a wee bit of privacy.

McDERMOT.   Marry me? *(Terrifying sound of breaking glass.)*

FRIEDA.   God!

McDERMOT.   That wasn't a Chinese gong. *(He leaps out of bed quickly and goes to the living room. Frieda follows him to the bedroom door, it looks immediately on to the hall.)*

FRIEDA.   *(Calling out.)* It's all your fault, John McDermot! I told you not to put up an election poster in the window.

McDERMOT.   *(Comes back. He is carrying a brick in one hand and a note in the other.)* Don't be such a harpy!

FRIEDA.   You called me a harpy! *(She snatches the note from him and reads. He sits down wearily on the bed and watches her.)* I expected this. Now do you believe me?

McDERMOT.   About what?

FRIEDA.   The man in the park.

McDERMOT.   Catch yourself on! *(She moves across the bedroom to the hall.)*

FRIEDA.   Time I was going.

McDERMOT.   Where to?

FRIEDA.   Safety. *(She drags a suitcase out of the hall.)*

McDERMOT.   I forgot, it's Sunday. You always run away on Sunday. *(She is packing clothes into the case.)* I thought you were banned from the ghetto.

FRIEDA.   I'm not going back there. I was thinking of leaving the tribes behind. Both of them!

McDERMOT.   Are you talking about leaving the country again?

FRIEDA.   Very definitely.

McDERMOT.   I ought to buy you a season ticket for the Liverpool boat. You pack that suitcase about three times a week. *(She continues packing.)* You'll be very unhappy. The Irish aren't popular where you're going. Thanks to your relatives.

FRIEDA.   You think I'm popular here? *(She indicates the brick.)*

72

Whatever England is — it's got to be better than this!

McDERMOT.   Oh, for heaven's sake! You're running away from a couple of drunks!

FRIEDA.   A couple of drunks?

McDERMOT.   Yes. A couple of drunks who've had their moment of power over you. Why give in to them?

FRIEDA.   I'm not so enamoured with my life here that it's something I could die defending.

McDERMOT.   Who said anything about dying?

FRIEDA.   It said in that note that this is a Protestant street! I have no wish to contest that. You have every right to live here. I haven't.

McDERMOT.   Frieda! Nobody in this street knows anything about you. The brick was thrown by a couple of mindless yobbos.

FRIEDA.   How do you know?

McDERMOT.   I teach those kids every day.

FRIEDA.   Oh please don't try to dismiss it just like that. You wouldn't believe me about the man in the rose gardens. And you wouldn't listen when I told you I felt watched every time I left the house. Now someone has put a brick through the front window! Please don't try to make out there's something wrong with me because I won't treat this as normal.

McDERMOT.   I'm not asking you to treat it as normal.

FRIEDA.   What's wrong, John? Are the Prods not allowed to be bad? *(She runs and picks up her case.)* I think you're becoming something of an apologist for your tribe. *(He leaps out of bed and slaps her across the head.)*

McDERMOT.   How dare you! *(In a rage, he hits her again.)* How dare you! *(Hits her again.)* I've spent my life fighting sectarianism. *(She falls into the corner, putting up her hands to protect her face and head. He hits out again.)*

FRIEDA.   Stop it! Please! *(He is standing over her breathing deeply, while she is crouched on the floor holding her head, unable and afraid to look up at him or move. He begins to pace the room.)*

McDERMOT.   My father was driven out of the shipyards thirty years ago. He was thrown from the deck of a ship by his workmates. When he plunged into the water he had to swim for his

73

life; they pelted him with rivets, spanners, crowbars, anything they had to hand. His tribe, my tribe, drove him out. And they did so because he tried to set up a union. He was a Protestant and a socialist. He was unemployed most of my life. Don't ever call me an apologist for my tribe again! *(She gets up and runs into the hall, where she bolts the door behind her. She sits' down on the floor with her head in her hands and weeps. McDermot comes to the door.)* Frieda! Open the door!

FRIEDA. *(Voice off. Shouts.)* No! I never want to see you again. *(McDermot begins to bang his head against the door, very hard. Several times. She is so frightened by this that she gets up and opens the door.)* Stop it! Please! Stop it!

McDERMOT. Don't shut me out! Don't leave me!

FRIEDA. But I can't stay here any more. I can't!

McDERMOT. If you leave me, I'll kill myself.

FRIEDA. If I stay, you'll kill me — or they will. *(He gets up and immediately bangs his head against the door again. Alarmed, she pulls him away to restrain him.)* All right. All right. I won't leave. But stop doing that! Please stop it!

McDERMOT. I love you, Frieda. I'll never let you go. I love you. *(He embraces her. She looks distressed.)*

Scene 9

Donna, Josie, Danny, Frieda, Malachy, Liam.

Donna's living room. The room is empty. Josie comes in, followed by Donna who is wearing only a dressing-gown and slippers.

JOSIE. I haven't seen you for so long, I was worried. Were you sleeping?

DONNA. What time is it?

JOSIE. It's not that late. You're not usually in bed at this time. When I was here we used to sit up all night. *(Danny appears.)*

DANNY. Hello, Josie.

JOSIE. Hi.

DANNY. I'll head away on. See you later. Good night. *(He exits.)*

DONNA. Are you staying? *(Pause.)* Is something wrong?

JOSIE. I'm not used to this. You might have told me!

DONNA. Like you told me about the baby? *(Josie sits down.)*

JOSIE. I saw Liam at the Club.

DONNA. Liam? What does he look like?

JOSIE. It's not his fault that he can't come home!

DONNA. No? But he can see other people.

JOSIE. Oh God. What a mess.

DONNA. *(Lighting a cigarette.)* Next time you see him, would you give him a message from me? Would you ask him to leave me alone?

JOSIE. You don't mean that.

DONNA. I do. I'm happy with Danny. He's young, he makes me feel innocent. *(Pause.)* Why didn't you tell me about the baby?

JOSIE. I tried to once. You rushed off.

DONNA. You should have come and told me. *(Donna sits.)* Did you want it?

JOSIE. I was surprised. It was a shock.

DONNA. What about Joe?

JOSIE. He's inscrutable. At first he wanted me to have an abortion so I'd be free.

DONNA. So that he could be free.

JOSIE. But now he's come around. He said he never thought he could make love to a pregnant woman.

DONNA. Is he away?

JOSIE. He's in Malta. He's due back tonight. I was too excited to sit in the house and wait on my own. And there were no women at the Club, so — I felt a bit prominent. *(They both laugh.)*

DONNA. Josie, I think you look beautiful. You suit a bit of weight on.

JOSIE. You know something, when he first came here, I wasn't sure about his motives. Then I realized that he had come to Ireland to win back his wife. I thought, I'm going to make this man love me.

DONNA. We all do desperate things when we're lonely.
JOSIE. *(Looking at herself.)* I'll never be lonely again! *(Frieda puts her head round the door.)*
FRIEDA. I was looking for a party. Did I come to the right place? *(They all stand and stare, then laugh.)*
JOSIE. Frieda!
DONNA. Look who it is! You're a stranger. *(Hugs Frieda.)*
FRIEDA. Look at you. *(Frieda hugs Josie.)*
JOSIE. You look great.
FRIEDA. *(To Josie.)* You look different. It's your face; it's fatter. No, it's not — I don't know what it is.
DONNA. She's pregnant.
FRIEDA. *(Pause.)* What did my daddy say?
JOSIE. Nothing.
FRIEDA. As bad as that? He's good at saying nothing.
JOSIE. No, really. He was OK. *(Donna excitedly goes off to the kitchen for glasses and a bottle.)*
FRIEDA. Well, tell me this, did you marry well?
JOSIE. Who's married?
FRIEDA. Look, I'm dying to ask. Is there a father?
JOSIE. Joe Conran.
FRIEDA. I always liked him. He's kinda shy.
DONNA. *(Returning.)* This calls for a celebration. *(She pours the new wine into a glass for each one.)*
FRIEDA. I thought I saw Danny McLoughlin from the top of the street.
DONNA. You just missed him.
FRIEDA. I think I did.
DONNA. So let's have a toast.
FRIEDA. To?
DONNA. To Josie's baby ... To Frieda's return ... To my love! *(They clink glasses and drink.)*
FRIEDA. Was it an accident?
DONNA. Frieda!
JOSIE. I wanted this.
FRIEDA. Did it matter who the father was?
JOSIE. I wouldn't have wanted it to be Cathal's child. *(Donna chokes on her wine, and looks in amasement at Josie.)* It's all right. I

can talk about it now.

FRIEDA. Sure everybody knew about you and Cathal O'Donnell. *(Drinks.)* Anyway, he's got nine kids already.

DONNA. Ten. She had a girl.

FRIEDA. She must be worn out.

DONNA. She's my age.

FRIEDA. She looks ten years older.

JOSIE. A child for every year ... that I knew him.

DONNA. *(To Frieda.)* What did you start!

JOSIE. I spoke to her once — a long time ago. It was just after I first saw her. She was suffering because of the heat. "He loves children," she said. "He's hoping for a boy this time." I tried to end it then. *(Donna pours more wine into Josie's glass.)*

DONNA. I don't think you should be drinking in your condition. *(They laugh. There is immediate hammering at the door. Springs to her feet and looks out of the window.)* That's your daddy! And you're not supposed to be here.

JOSIE. You could hide in the kitchen.

FRIEDA. No! *(She stands up with her arms folded and waits. Donna lets Malachy into the room. He seems in a hurry. He stops at the sight of Frieda, then turns to Josie.)*

MALACHY. Are you fit to travel?

JOSIE. I'm pregnant, Daddy, I'm not an invalid!

MALACHY. I've come to take you away with me now.

JOSIE. Why?

MALACHY. The *Sea Fern* was met as soon as it entered Irish waters — before the fishing fleet could get to her and before the crew could dump the cargo.

JOSIE. Who met her?

MALACHY. Irish security police — they were tipped off this afternoon by the British Government. Our contact in the Guarda said the shipment was betrayed in Valetta. The British had been following its progress since it left Malta.

JOSIE. *(Suddenly alarmed.)* Jesus! God! What's happened to Joe?

MALACHY. Josie! It was Joe who betrayed us! Everybody's saying it. I've come to take you away with me.

JOSIE. Who's saying it?

MALACHY. Ask Liam.

JOSIE. Liam's down on Joe. What does Cathal say?

MALACHY. Cathal is stubborn enough to believe that Joe Conran is coming back — he insists on waiting for him at the rendezvous.

JOSIE. *(Relieved.)* Believe Cathal.

MALACHY. Listen. Joe's coming back isn't proof of his innocence.

JOSIE. The capture of the *Sea Fern* is not proof of Joe's guilt. We've lost shipments before!

MALACHY. If Conran is a British agent they'll be looking for us and everyone he's met.

JOSIE. Joe would not betray me! I've lived with him. I know him. I'm carrying his child. Do you not think I would know? *(Hammering at the door. Everyone freezes.)*

DONNA. *(Looks out of the window.)* Liam.

MALACHY. Go on, girl. Open the door! *(Donna moves quickly to the door, admitting Liam.)* What's happened, son?

LIAM. *(Starts suddenly at the sight of Frieda.)* What's she doing here?

MALACHY. Who?

LIAM. Frieda! She's standing right behind you!

MALACHY. I don't see anyone. What's wrong, for Christ's sake!

LIAM. Gabriel drove out of the hospital tonight with a van load of supplies. He was stopped by the police. He showed them his forged security pass and told them he was delivering provisions to the Nurses' Home.

MALACHY. At this time of night?

LIAM. They let him go. He drove the stuff straight to the Club as usual.

MALACHY. What — the pin head!

LIAM. Of course, he didn't know the police were following him. They arrested him and everybody on the premises for handling stolen goods. O'Donnell was among the people arrested. *(Slightly turning in Donna's way and then back.)* So was that musician, Danny McLoughlin. He'd just walked in.

MALACHY. Holy Jesus! *(Donna crosses the room to where Josie is standing.)*

DONNA. How come you got away?

LIAM. I wasn't on the premises.

JOSIE. How do you know all this?

LIAM. Eileen Watterson told me. She's a barmaid at the Club.

MALACHY. Now do you believe me?

JOSIE. This is pure chance!

LIAM. It was a cover for a raid.

JOSIE. Joe would not betray me!

LIAM. He's not coming back!

JOSIE. I don't believe it.

LIAM. Josie. He got what he came for. Eileen told me they went straight to O'Donnell. They even had a layout of the Club. And they knew what he looked like.

JOSIE. No. No. No!

LIAM. How many months pregnant are you?

JOSIE. Three.

LIAM. Kill it. I want you to kill the child!

JOSIE. Why?

LIAM. The father is a traitor. He did not love you; he used you. It's better that his child should not be born at all.

JOSIE. But it's my baby — it doesn't matter about anything else.

LIAM. It's his child!

DONNA. No. It's not, Liam. It's what you never understood. A child doesn't belong to anyone. It's itself. *(Liam grabs Josie's arms.)*

LIAM. Do it. Don't force us!

JOSIE. *(In terror.)* No!

MALACHY. Take your hands off her! *(Liam lets go of Josie's arm.)* I'm the father here, son!

LIAM. What's wrong with you? She's carrying Conran's baby! *(Malachy puts his arm round Josie.)*

MALACHY. My baby now. *(Pause while he looks around.)* Josie's going to live with me from now on. Isn't that right, love?

JOSIE. *(Hesitant.)* Yes.

MALACHY. This baby's my blood. If anyone harms a hair on its head...!

LIAM. You're an old man, Malachy. *(Malachy begins to move through the room to the door, leading Josie away with him.)*
MALACHY. I'll be twice as long as you, son! *(Malachy opens the door.)* Now Josie and I are going to take a wee trip away from all this attention — I advise you three to do the same. The soldiers will be here before long. *(He leads Josie away.)*
DONNA. Josie! *(She does not turn round. They exit.)*
LIAM. I have to make tracks. *(Liam prepares to leave.)*
DONNA. Liam!
LIAM. I can't stay, Donna. They'll be looking for me. I couldn't go back in there.
DONNA. I'll be here.
LIAM. I'd prefer if she wasn't!
FRIEDA. I came to say good-bye to my sisters, I wasn't intending to stay.
DONNA. *(To Liam.)* Come back when it's safe. *(Liam appears to want to embrace Donna, but she isn't encouraging. He thinks better of it, and waves quickly.)*
FRIEDA. Why don't you leave him! *(They sit on the sofa.)*
DONNA. *(Mildly surprised.)* Why? How?
FRIEDA. You're not happy.
DONNA. I think I may have lost the capacity for happiness. I left my son for him. I thought if I had another it would make it up. But it didn't. As soon as I conceived I noticed the change. I lost my desire. All my life I felt I had to run fast, seek, look, struggle for things and hold on to things or lose them, but as soon as I felt the child inside me again, the baby quickening, I knew that it was coming and there was nothing I could do. I felt for the first time the course of things, the inevitability. And I thought, no, I won't struggle any more, I shall just do. And all that time longing — was wasted, because life just turns things out as they are. Happiness, sadness, has really nothing to do with it. *(A child begins to cry upstairs. Donna listens. Frieda makes a move to go.)*
DONNA. Don't go yet.
FRIEDA. I'll stay until it's light. *(The crying stops.)*
DONNA. She has wee dreams. I'll bring her down if she cries again. *(Pause.)* So you're saying good-bye.

FRIEDA. *(Nods.)* I left him sleeping. I walked out just as I am. If I'd taken a suitcase he'd have known and stopped me.

DONNA. Have you somewhere to go?

FRIEDA. England.

DONNA. Why England?

FRIEDA. Why not? It's my language.

DONNA. Why not go South?

FRIEDA. I'm not that kind of Irish.

DONNA. It didn't work out then?

FRIEDA. No.

DONNA. Any reason?

FRIEDA. Different commitments.

DONNA. It'll be lonely.

FRIEDA. I'd rather be lonely than suffocate.

DONNA. I understand, but it only lasts a little while that feeling. As you get older, companionship is very important. Filling the space in the bed with someone. Preferably a good friend.

FRIEDA. I want to write songs.

DONNA. Write to me.

FRIEDA. If I have anything to say. *(Pause. Looks away from Donna straight ahead.)* I remember a long time ago, a moonlit night on a beach below the Mournes, we were having a late summer barbecue on the shore at Tyrella. Among the faces at the fire were Josie, Donna, Liam, and my father and mother were there too. And John McDermot was a friend of Liam's.

DONNA. I remember.

FRIEDA. We three slipped off from the campfire to swim leaving the men arguing on the beach. And Donna said, "I'm going to marry Liam McCoy one day." And we all laughed. And I said, "Well then, I'll marry John McDermot." And we sank down into the calm water and tried to catch the phosphorescence on the surface of the waves — it was the first time I'd ever seen it — and the moon was reflected on the sea that night. It was as though we swam in the night sky and cupped the stars between our cool fingers. And then they saw us. First Liam and then John, and my father in a temper because we'd left our swimsuits on the beach. And the shouting and the slapping and the waves breaking over us. We raced for cover to an-

81

other part of the shore. We escaped into the shadows and were clothed again before they reached us. We lay down in the sand-hills and laughed.

DONNA. I remember.

FRIEDA. I have not thought of that night for many years.

DONNA. *(Looking out.)* The sky's getting lighter.

FRIEDA. Oh, it's not him; it is Ireland I am leaving.

DONNA. How quietly the light comes. *(Darkness.)*

PROPERTY LIST

Paper (FRIEDA)
Boxes (GABRIEL, FIRST MAN)
Hanky (DONNA)
Bottle of wine and 3 glasses (DONNA)
Couple of quid (MALACHY)
Traveling bag (JOE)
Packet of cigarettes(JOE, O'DONNELL)
Cups of coffee (DONNA)
Bottle of whiskey and 2 glasses (FRIEDA)
Towel (DONNA)
File (JOSIE)
Shoulder bag (JOSIE)
Wallet (JOE)
Notes (JOE)
Match (MALACHY)
Cigarette (O'DONNELL, DONNA)
Knife (DONNA)
Armful of dresses on hangers (JOSIE)
Handful of leaflets (FRIEDA)
Suitcase (FRIEDA)
Notebook (McDERMOTT)
2 small firearms in a towel (SECOND SOLDIER)
Piece of paper (POLICEMAN)
Pint glasses (MALACHY, LIAM)
Brick (McDERMOTT)
Note (McDERMOTT)
Suitcase (FRIEDA)

SOUND EFFECTS

Footsteps
Footsteps clattering in the alley
Bin lids hammering
Helicoptor
Doorbell
Footsteps on the stairs
Door banging
Phone ringing
Landrover screeching to a halt
Car door slamming
Young child crying
Heavily shod feet running
Cacophony of cymbals, skin drums, and tambourines from
    the street
Breaking glass
Hammering at the door

NEW PLAYS

★ **CLOSER by Patrick Marber.** Winner of the 1998 Olivier Award for Best Play and the 1999 New York Drama Critics Circle Award for Best Foreign Play. Four lives intertwine over the course of four and a half years in this densely plotted, stinging look at modern love and betrayal. "CLOSER is a sad, savvy, often funny play that casts a steely, unblinking gaze at the world of relationships and lets you come to your own conclusions ... CLOSER does not merely hold your attention; it burrows into you." –*New York Magazine* "A powerful, darkly funny play about the cosmic collision between the sun of love and the comet of desire." –*Newsweek Magazine* [2M, 2W] ISBN: 0-8222-1722-8

★ **THE MOST FABULOUS STORY EVER TOLD by Paul Rudnick.** A stage manager, headset and prompt book at hand, brings the house lights to half, then dark, and cues the creation of the world. Throughout the play, she's in control of everything. In other words, she's either God, or she thinks she is. "Line by line, Mr. Rudnick may be the funniest writer for the stage in the United States today ... One-liners, epigrams, withering put-downs and flashing repartee: These are the candles that Mr. Rudnick lights instead of cursing the darkness ... a testament to the virtues of laughing ... and in laughter, there is something like the memory of Eden." –*The NY Times* "Funny it is ... consistently, rapaciously, deliriously ... easily the funniest play in town." –*Variety* [4M, 5W] ISBN: 0-8222-1720-1

★ **A DOLL'S HOUSE by Henrik Ibsen, adapted by Frank McGuinness.** Winner of the 1997 Tony Award for Best Revival. "New, raw, gut-twisting and gripping. Easily the hottest drama this season." –*USA Today* "Bold, brilliant and alive." –*The Wall Street Journal* "A thunderclap of an evening that takes your breath away." –*Time Magazine* [4M, 4W, 2 boys] ISBN: 0-8222-1636-1

★ **THE HERBAL BED by Peter Whelan.** The play is based on actual events which occurred in Stratford-upon-Avon in the summer of 1613, when William Shakespeare's daughter was publicly accused of having a sexual liaison with a married neighbor and family friend. "In his probing new play, THE HERBAL BED ... Peter Whelan muses about a sidelong event in the life of Shakespeare's family and creates a finely textured tapestry of love and lies in the early 17th-century Stratford." –*The NY Times* "It is a first rate drama with interesting moral issues of truth and expediency." –*The NY Post* [5M, 3W] ISBN: 0-8222-1675-2

★ **SNAKEBIT by David Marshall Grant.** A study of modern friendship when put to the test. "... a rather smart and absorbing evening of water-cooler theater, the intimate sort of Off-Broadway experience that has you picking apart the recognizable characters long after the curtain calls." – *The NY Times* "Off-Broadway keeps on presenting us with compelling reasons for going to the theater. The latest is SNAKEBIT, David Marshall Grant's smart new comic drama about being thirtysomething and losing one's way in life." –*The NY Daily News* [3M, 1W] ISBN: 0-8222-1724-4

★ **A QUESTION OF MERCY by David Rabe.** The Obie Award-winning playwright probes the sensitive and controversial issue of doctor-assisted suicide in the age of AIDS in this poignant drama. "There are many devastating ironies in Mr. Rabe's beautifully considered, piercingly clear-eyed work ..." –*The NY Times* "With unsettling candor and disturbing insight, the play arouses pity and understanding of a troubling subject ... Rabe's provocative tale is an affirmation of dignity that rings clear and true." –*Variety* [6M, 1W] ISBN: 0-8222-1643-4

★ **DIMLY PERCEIVED THREATS TO THE SYSTEM by Jon Klein.** Reality and fantasy overlap with hilarious results as this unforgettable family attempts to survive the nineties. "Here's a play whose point about fractured families goes to the heart, mind – and ears." –*The Washington Post* "... an end-of-the millennium comedy about a family on the verge of a nervous breakdown ... Trenchant and hilarious ..." –*The Baltimore Sun* [2M, 4W] ISBN: 0-8222-1677-9

DRAMATISTS PLAY SERVICE, INC.
440 Park Avenue South, New York, NY 10016 212-683-8960 Fax 212-213-1539
postmaster@dramatists.com www.dramatists.com

NEW PLAYS

★ **AS BEES IN HONEY DROWN by Douglas Carter Beane.** Winner of the John Gassner Playwriting Award. A hot young novelist finds the subject of his new screenplay in a New York socialite who leads him into the world of *Auntie Mame* and *Breakfast at Tiffany's*, before she takes him for a ride. "A delicious soufflé of a satire … [an] extremely entertaining fable for an age that always chooses image over substance." *—The NY Times* "… A witty assessment of one of the most active and relentless industries in a consumer society … the creation of 'hot' young things, which the media have learned to mass produce with efficiency and zeal." *—The NY Daily News* [3M, 3W, flexible casting] ISBN: 0-8222-1651-5

★ **STUPID KIDS by John C. Russell.** In rapid, highly stylized scenes, the story follows four high-school students as they make their way from first through eighth period and beyond, struggling with the fears, frustrations, and longings peculiar to youth. "In STUPID KIDS … playwright John C. Russell gets the opera of adolescence to a T … The stylized teenspeak of STUPID KIDS … suggests that Mr. Russell may have hidden a tape recorder under a desk in study hall somewhere and then scoured the tapes for good quotations … it is the kids' insular, ceaselessly churning world, a pre-adult world of Doritos and libidos, that the playwright seeks to lay bare." *—The NY Times* "STUPID KIDS [is] a sharp-edged … whoosh of teen angst and conformity anguish. It is also very funny." *—NY Newsday* [2M, 2W] ISBN: 0-8222-1698-1

★ **COLLECTED STORIES by Donald Margulies.** From Obie Award-winner Donald Margulies comes a provocative analysis of a student-teacher relationship that turns sour when the protégé becomes a rival. "With his fine ear for detail, Margulies creates an authentic, insular world, and he gives equal weight to the opposing viewpoints of two formidable characters." *—The LA Times* "This is probably Margulies' best play to date …" *—The NY Post* "… always fluid and lively, the play is thick with ideas, like a stock-pot of good stew." *—The Village Voice* [2W] ISBN: 0-8222-1640-X

★ **FREEDOMLAND by Amy Freed.** An overdue showdown between a son and his father sets off fireworks that illuminate the neurosis, rage and anxiety of one family – and of America at the turn of the millennium. "FREEDOMLAND's more obvious links are to *Buried Child* and *Bosoms and Neglect*. Freed, like Guare, is an inspired wordsmith with a gift for surreal touches in situations grounded in familiar and real territory." *—Curtain Up* [3M, 4W] ISBN: 0-8222-1719-8

★ **STOP KISS by Diana Son.** A poignant and funny play about the ways, both sudden and slow, that lives can change irrevocably. "There's so much that is vital and exciting about STOP KISS … you want to embrace this young author and cheer her onto other works … the writing on display here is funny and credible … you also will be charmed by its heartfelt characters and up-to-the-minute humor." *—The NY Daily News* "… irresistibly exciting … a sweet, sad, and enchantingly sincere play." *—The NY Times* [3M, 3W] ISBN: 0-8222-1731-7

★ **THREE DAYS OF RAIN by Richard Greenberg.** The sins of fathers and mothers make for a bittersweet elegy in this poignant and revealing drama. "… a work so perfectly judged it heralds the arrival of a major playwright … Greenberg is extraordinary." *—The NY Daily News* "Greenberg's play is filled with graceful passages that are by turns melancholy, harrowing, and often, quite funny." *—Variety* [2M, 1W] ISBN: 0-8222-1676-0

★ **THE WEIR by Conor McPherson.** In a bar in rural Ireland, the local men swap spooky stories in an attempt to impress a young woman from Dublin who recently moved into a nearby "haunted" house. However, the tables are soon turned when she spins a yarn of her own. "You shed all sense of time at this beautiful and devious new play." *—The NY Times* "Sheer theatrical magic. I have rarely been so convinced that I have just seen a modern classic. Tremendous." *—The London Daily Telegraph* [4M, 1W] ISBN: 0-8222-1706-6

DRAMATISTS PLAY SERVICE, INC.
440 Park Avenue South, New York, NY 10016 212-683-8960 Fax 212-213-1539
postmaster@dramatists.com www.dramatists.com